"Diane continuously delivers serious content with energetic wit. She knows how to captivate an audience and keep them engaged. Her no-nonsense feedback charming manner, and 'tell it like it is' approach is fresh, relatable and authentic. She deeply cares about empowering others and inspires them to do the same. Her tips are always current, practical and timeless, and she is 'the real deal.'"

— Nicole Van Den Heuvel, Director, Center for Career Development, Rice University

"Never fussy, always approachable, Diane Gottsman's insights in the realm of etiquette are compelling and right on-point. With the trifecta of research, intuition and a true passion for her subject, she has created another winner—a book that's a must-read for anyone seeking to achieve more effective (and considerate) interactions with others."

— Thomas P. Farley, A.K.A. Mister Manners, Modern Manners and Business Etiquette Expert

Modern
Etiquette
for a
Better Life

Master All Social and Business Exchanges

Diane Gottsman

America's Go-To Etiquette Expert

The Protocol School of Texas

PAGE STREET
PUBLISHING CO.

PAGE STREET
PUBLISHING CO.

First published in 2017 by
Page Street Publishing Co.
27 Congress Street, Suite 105
Salem, MA 01970
www.pagestreetpublishing.com

Distributed by Macmillan, sales in Canada by The Canadian Manda Group.

19 18 17 16   1 2 3 4

ISBN-13: 978-1-62414-325-0
ISBN-10: 1-62414-325-3

Library of Congress Control Number: 2016953999

Cover and book design by Page Street Publishing Co.
Illustrations by Robert Brandt

Printed and bound in China

To my dad, who left this world too early, but not before showing me the importance of kindness, strength, bravery, respect and most of all, love.

Contents

Section 1: Conquering Business from the Break Room to the Boardroom   11

Section 2: The Delicate Art of a Powerful Business Meal   79

Section 3: Social Skills That Dazzle and Shine   105

Introduction

My interest in civility and the responsibility that is required to function in a world that is often harsh and cold goes back to completing a master's degree in sociology and aspiring to interact with underprivileged youth. I found myself working in a children's shelter where babies and young kids would arrive in the back of a police car, in need of care and shelter while their parents were taken off to jail. Saddened by their circumstances, I was enamored with their strong spirit. I also began to observe a common thread among the older kids— they didn't feel worthy. One day, while I was working at the shelter, a sweet eleven-year-old girl commented, "When I grow up I want to be rich like you." I asked her why she thought I was rich and she said, "Your shoes are always so shiny." It struck me . . . these kids desperately needed self-confidence and this young girl needed to know she wasn't limited and could achieve whatever she wanted, regardless of her current situation or socioeconomic level. I suddenly had a plan and I didn't look back. For the past seventeen years, I have had the pleasure of working with university students, corporate executives, nonprofits and CEOs on honing their executive leadership skills. The reality is, it's impossible to go through life without experiencing a myriad of awkward moments along the way. My intention in writing this book is to empower you and offer suggestions on how to best respond in both the business and social arena. Whether it's a cocktail party, a formal dinner, asking for a raise or surviving a layoff, you'll find quick tips that are user-friendly and can be immediately put into use. Life is better when you know what to do next! Etiquette skills in their truest form are about making others comfortable. When you are feeling confident, it shows in your behavior and how you treat other people. The sign of a leader is someone who is capable of conquering sticky situations and putting others at ease. Leaders know how to build genuine relationships and encourage an authentic feeling of trust. When people trust you, they become your closest friends, most loyal clients and strongest advocates. My definition of etiquette is being brave enough to align your words with your actions. Regardless of your wealth . . . money doesn't buy class, only a great pair of shiny shoes. Are you ready to put your best foot forward?

Conquering Business from the Break Room to the Boardroom

Networking

Network Like a Pro

Walking through the door of a busy networking event is enough to make most people want to turn and run the other way. By sticking to some basic rules, you will not only survive the experience but thrive while meeting and impressing new connections.

A study conducted nearly a century ago by the Carnegie Foundation found that soft skills (productive interpersonal people skills) make for a whopping 85 percent of a person's success. Today, in our technology-driven business world, soft skills matter more than ever. If yours are lacking or lagging behind, put these tips into practice.

Remember: You're not there to close a deal. Attending a networking function is, at its very core, an opportunity to build relationships. Set a goal to meet five to ten new people, depending on the size of the event.

Where do you begin? The perfect greeting starts with your feet. Men and women show professional presence by standing up. Staying seated tells the other person he or she is not worth the extra effort to rise. When one person stands and the other stays seated, it's clear who holds the power.

The Perfect Handshake

The formula for a successful handshake is a firm, confident grip, making contact with the other person's palm. Keep your elbow slightly bent and extend your hand. Shake three or four times and let go.

The perfect handshake will leave a good impression and open doors.

Avoid the following ill-fated grips:

The Preaching Politician

A double-fisted grasp is too personal for an initial introduction. Reserve this gesture for those you know well. It is also considered a familial or condolence handshake.

The Frat Bump

Unless you are a coach on the sports field, straighten your suit jacket and unfold your fingers for an executive shake.

The Clammy Cod Fish

Men often lighten up so they won't hurt the female professional with their "manly" grip. The result is a soft, insecure physical greeting. Women sometimes do the same because they were taught as young girls to "shake like a lady." The result is a disastrous introduction that is hard to forget.

The Lobster Claw

Imagine feeling the clench of a sharp, unpleasant pinch. This handshake signals a person is forceful and headstrong. No one enjoys shaking hands with a bully.

Giving Someone the Finger

Don't allow your index finger to extend up the wrist of the other person's arm. It's an invasive sensation that can easily be avoided by rolling your pointer finger around the hand of the other person.

The Preaching Politician

The Frat Bump

The Clammy Cod Fish

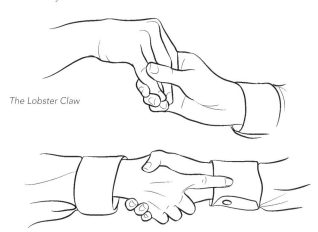

The Lobster Claw

Giving Someone the Finger

You Are There to Meet, Not Eat

Dinner Can Wait

Have a snack before leaving your office, so you don't arrive with a grumbling stomach and an insatiable desire to load up on the shrimp cocktail.

"Dishing up" will most certainly eat away at valuable time meeting new clients or fine-tuning your relationships with associates and colleagues you don't see on a regular basis. When possible, learn who will be in attendance and make a mental list of those you'd like to meet before the night is over.

Lean Left

Not physically, but in your mind. Remember to carry your plate or drink in your left hand, ready for the onslaught of handshakes you will encounter in a large group of people. Do not attempt a balancing act with your plate, wineglass and dessert. Juggling multiple items while socializing is a recipe for disaster.

Introductions

When meeting someone new, always offer your first and last name. Giving only your first name is equivalent to sending an email and omitting the signature line. Stating your full name is a sign of confidence, respect and professionalism. The same rule applies in social settings.

The Eyes Have It

There's a reason for the popular phrase "seeing eye to eye" or "the eyes are the window to your soul." Maintaining eye contact shows you're listening and interested. Glancing around the room suggests you'd rather be elsewhere.

Smile . . . Lights, Camera, Action

Think about it. Are you motivated to approach people who are wearing a scowl, standing with their arms crossed? This person has an unfortunate case of "cranky resting face." They may not even realize why people stay at arm's length.

Adopt the opposite body language to set yourself up for a friendly networking experience. Smile broadly, separate your lips slightly and allow your eyes to crease. People will notice the "twinkle" and be grateful for a friendly face.

The Highs and Hazards of Hugging

Maybe you've met people with whom you hit it off professionally, and you are impressed with their warm social demeanor. You connect as if you've known them for years. When it comes time to say good-bye, a handshake feels too formal and you want to give them a big, friendly bear hug. What to do?

Resist the urge! In business, the only professional greeting is a handshake. However, there are exceptions. A hug is acceptable when you have developed a close relationship, and your client stretches out his or her arms first. It would be rude to stick your hand in the stomach of someone who is closing in for an embrace. But, fair warning, if this is a first-time meeting, regardless of the kismet, err on the side of caution and end your conversation hand to hand.

Business Card Basics

Even in today's hyperconnected world, business cards have an important role. Yours should help reinforce your professionalism; opt for a classic layout on a heavyweight card stock from a reputable print company.

When exchanging business cards with someone you've just met, there are things you should do, as well as things you should avoid.

Do

- Invest in a quality leather card case for a nice impression and to keep business cards from getting soiled or damaged.
- The senior executive should present his or her card first.
- Hand your card with the print facing upward so the recipient can easily read it.
- The recipient should take the card, look at it, make a comment and then place it in a jacket pocket or purse.
- Present a card to the receptionist when entering an office.
- When conducting business abroad, prepare business cards with the client's native language on one side and an English version on the other. Hand the card to the recipient with the country's native language facing up.

Don't

- Offer a soiled or bent card.
- Fail to have new cards reprinted should your contact information change.
- Hand out cards at a social event.
- As a junior executive, ask a senior executive for a card.
- Put a card in your pants pocket, shirtsleeve or cuff.
- Write notes on a card in front of the other person (do so later).

Look Alive and Listen

Multitasking is the way of the world. We quickly check our email during a meeting or update to-do lists at the end of a call. Juggling demanding schedules, packed with work and personal obligations, has become the norm. As a result, listening and retaining the information we hear is increasingly difficult.

But listening is a key tenet in business communication. Mastery of this skill will serve you well in both your career and your personal life.

Clear Your Mind

When you arrive somewhere to meet others, whether it's mingling over cocktails or introducing yourself before a conference, focus on the present. Push mental clutter, such as a reminder to pick up milk and dry cleaning on the way home, out of your mind. In this moment, you have one purpose: not just to hear what others are saying, but to truly internalize it.

Commit Names to Memory

Repeat people's names in the introduction and again during the conversation when it makes sense. Utilize their name tag for a quick reference. If in the middle of a conversation, you have forgotten their name, simply own it. Say, "Forgive me, I'm going blank. Please remind me of your name once again." You can also use this tactic when you encounter someone you know but can't quickly recall his or her name.

A name tag is worn on the right shoulder to follow the line of sight from a handshake.

Take It Slow

Rushing through a conversation increases the likelihood you won't remember key points after the fact. Concentrate on the individual in front of you and ask open-ended questions. Inquire further. Rather than constantly pushing on to the next topic, allow time to get to know the person better and learn something in depth.

Respond but Don't Interrupt

A few thoughtful comments ("I agree" or even a simple "mm-hmm") go a long way, both in showing the other person that you're interested and that you're on the same page. Interject where needed, but don't halt another person mid-thought.

Minimize Distractions

Stand away from the door, the bar or busy thoroughfare and avoid scanning the room to see who else you know. Face the person you're speaking to, with your shoulders parallel, and make direct eye contact.

When in Doubt, Repeat and Rephrase

Paraphrasing or restating what someone already said reiterates that you understand. But it can also help you remember what you've heard and recall that fact later on. Use this tactic as another way to propel the chat deeper. For example, rather than "Oh, you went to the University of Missouri? One of my colleagues is an alumnus," try taking it in a different direction, à la "What did you major in at Mizzou? Were you part of any clubs on campus?" Chances are, when you see that person again, you'll be able to recollect the details.

Small Talk Is Big Business

Avoid a rehearsed "schmooze." It's your job to be interesting, and you must put in the work. Be knowledgeable about current events, the latest movies, sports and local happenings. Ask open-ended questions and listen more than you speak. The more you allow someone else to share, the better a conversationalist you become!

Exit Stage Door Left

Don't monopolize someone's time. Spend five to ten minutes chatting and then move along. Simply say, "It was nice meeting you," or "I really enjoyed our visit, and I hope to talk again soon." Don't use the filler excuse, "I will call you for lunch soon" unless you intend to do so.

Executive Wardrobe Suggestions for Him

Basic wardrobe items offer a variety of options for the professional man. A few key pieces will get you through a week of business meetings and after-hour events.

- Suits: navy, charcoal gray, dark gray pinstripe
- Sport Jackets: navy, herringbone
- Dress Slacks: navy, charcoal, tan

- "Casual Friday"
  - Khakis
  - Dark washed jeans
  - Polo-style golf shirt or Oxford shirt
  - Belt/loafers
  - V-neck sweaters: gray, navy
- Socks
  - Calf length (match the slacks)
  - Colorful—alternate choice to show off your personality
- Dress Shirts
  - 3 white (1 button-down Oxford)
  - 2 light blue
  - 1 blue button-down Oxford
- Belts
  - Black and brown leather
- Shoes
  - Cap-toe black lace-up
  - Brown wing-tip to be worn with a suit
  - Leather loafer (casual)
- Coats (Weather)
  - Single-breasted wool coat
  - All-weather trench coat
  - Double-breasted pea coat
- Umbrella
- The Suit: Executive Staple
  - An all-season fabric is the most versatile choice.
  - The best option is 100 percent wool, tropical or medium weight.
  - Avoid cotton blends and linen (which wrinkle easily) and polyester blends (which are not as durable).
  - A black suit is not flattering on everyone.

- **The Sport Coat: Professional**
  - Does not require a tie and can be layered with a vest in cooler weather.
- **The Button Golden Rule**
  - The top button is **sometimes** buttoned.
  - The middle button is **always** buttoned.
  - The bottom button is **never** buttoned.
- **Dress Shirts**
  - The best option is 100 percent cotton, as it breathes and absorbs moisture.
  - Dress shirt fabrics typically come in broadcloth (smooth, silky finish) or Oxford (rougher finish, less formal, used in button-down styles).
- **Shirt Colors**
  - Solid white sends the most powerful message.
  - Light blue tones are second in command.
  - Pastels convey an "approachable" vibe.
- **The Shirt Collar**
  - Tab: worn with a suit or tie.
  - Button-down: worn with business casual attire.
- **Shirt Cuffs**
  - Barrel cuffs have one or two buttons, and should extend ¼ inch (6 mm) below the coat or jacket sleeve.
  - French cuffs require cuff links, and should extend ½ inch (13 mm) below the coat or jacket sleeve.
  - Short sleeves should be reserved for casual wear.
- **The Tie**
  - Vary solids, stripes, pin dots and small patterns.
- **The Trouser**
  - Worn with a sport coat and a button-down shirt. When seated, the ankle should not be exposed.

A modern man's business casual look.

Executive Wardrobe Suggestions for Her

A successful businesswoman knows the value of making a powerful statement through her choice of clothing. Check your closet for the following basics.

- Dress: Sheath or Wrap
    - Basic black (LBD, a.k.a., little black dress)
    - Variety of colors
    - With and without sleeves

- White cotton shirt—timeless
- Cashmere sweater
- Blouse: for slacks or skirts
- Jacket: for slacks or skirts
- Layering camisole/tank/underpinning
- Shoes
    - Classic heel: nude, black
    - Ballerina-style flats
    - Brown or black riding boots
- The Suit: A Smart Investment
    - An all-season fabric is the most versatile choice.
    - Lightweight wool, gabardine or wool blend are good options.
    - Avoid linen and polyester-rayon blends.
- The Blouse
    - Suitable fabric options include silk, crepe and cotton.
    - The blouse front should be open no lower than 1 inch (2.5 mm) above the cleavage.
    - The sleeve should reach the wrist bone and extend from the jacket ⅛ to ¼ inch (3 to 6 mm).
    - Sleeveless shirts may be worn under a suit jacket.
- The Trouser: Select a Flattering Cut for Your Body Type
- The Skirt: Should be Comfortable While Sitting, Standing and Bending
- A Sweater Set
    - Appropriate when a suit is not required
    - Can replace a jacket, worn over a dress or under a blazer
    - Is a good travel option

Choose a heel that you can easily walk in.

- Shoes
    - Classic pumps that can be rotated throughout the week
    - **Avoid** strappy sandals and extreme heels.
    - Flip-flops and beach sandals don't belong at the office.

Modern Etiquette for a Better Life

- Hosiery:
    - Refer to your company handbook and follow its policy. Most offices are fairly lenient, but there are some industries where hosiery is a must.
    - Neutral shades are the most professional and flattering.
    - **Avoid** patterned or textured hosiery in a conservative environment.
- Makeup: Not Optional for Those Climbing the Corporate Ladder.
    - It adds expression to your face and shows you take pride in yourself.
    - Essentials include natural color foundation, blush and lipstick or gloss.
    - Keep your makeup subtle and avoid heavy bronzer during the day.
- Purse
    - Cross-body bag (great for travel)
    - Leather tote
    - Wallet clutch
- Coats
    - All-weather trench coat
    - Wool midcalf coat
    - Short car coat
- Jewelry
    - Statement necklace
    - Pearl earrings
    - Gold hoops
- Tights/Shapewear
- Umbrella

In the Workplace

8 Things You Should Never Say at a Business Function

It's embarrassing enough when you stick your foot in your mouth among friends, but the stakes get higher when you say something foolish in front of a boss, client or peer at a meeting, business dinner or conference.

It wouldn't be a stretch to say your verbal misstep may have lasting repercussions. Keeping things professional doesn't mean you have to sound robotic or overly formal. It simply requires you to think before you speak, and avoid phrases that could be misinterpreted as childish, dismissive or combative.

1. "That's impossible."

In general, bosses want employees who are flexible, goal-oriented and positive. When asked whether you can meet a deadline or spearhead a challenging project, you want to manage expectations without completely shooting down the suggestion. "Are you kidding? That's impossible!" comes across less admirably than, "John, that's quite an ambitious timeline. May I check my calendar to see what other projects are pending? I will get back to you this afternoon." You have now bought yourself some time to gather your thoughts, come up with a plan and brainstorm alternative suggestions.

2. "Rough night?"

Whether a co-worker looks as if he or she has worked all night, danced until three a.m. or stayed up with a sick infant, do not specifically mention the individual's bedraggled or otherwise haggard appearance. If you're both waiting for coffee to brew in the kitchen, and you have a friendly dynamic, you can ask, "Claire, are you feeling okay? You don't quite look like yourself." Use a sincerely sympathetic tone of voice to show concern. You colleague may need an ear, or is now forewarned that he or she may want to freshen up.

3. "I think . . ." or "I feel . . ."

When you're presenting an idea or making a case for a project, there's no need to attach your emotions to the facts. Go with a straightforward statement, such as "This report will give us the clear guidelines we need to make a sound decision," rather than "It's my humble opinion that we need this report." The second scenario is less sure and not nearly as authoritative as the first. Back your statement up with facts rather than opinions. Your teammates will respect you more for it.

4. "When are you due?"

To be clear, there are a handful of times this phrase is deemed acceptable: First, after a co-worker has informed you that she is expecting and has also made clear that the exciting announcement is public knowledge in the workplace. Second, at an office-wide baby shower honoring the soon-to-be mommy co-worker. And third, when the mother-to-be's due date is imminent, and she is enthusiastically counting down the days.

At no other time should this question be uttered in a business setting. Do not make any assumptions about a co-worker's weight gain or other physical changes. Even if it seems obvious, unless your co-worker mentions it first, stick to the reason you are meeting and refrain from asking any questions, including "When are you due?" It is as rude and invasive to reach out and pat an expectant mother's belly.

5. "I'm sorry."

Women, in particular, fall into the habit (or, rather, the trap) of apologizing for various reasons in the workplace. If you find yourself in this vicious cycle, practice cutting the phrase from your professional vocabulary. Instead of "I'm sorry to bother you, but . . ." say, "Excuse me, do you have a minute?" More often than not, "sorry" is just a filler word and whatever you're about to say will sound more powerful without it.

6. "You look nothing like I expected . . ."

If your relationship with a client or a colleague from a different office began over the phone or email, guard against making assumptions about physical appearance. Whether you found contacts on LinkedIn or some other social media site, mentioning they are several years older than their profile picture is never a good start to a relationship. While it may work to your advantage to say they are younger than you imagined, it's not worth the risk and you may come across as insincere.

7. "What a great outfit!"

While you might feel this is perfectly acceptable at the water cooler or in the elevator, don't bring up clothing, jewelry or hair at a business meeting. If you're dying to know where your client gets her highlights, hold the question for a moment where you're one-on-one. The etiquette regarding a business compliment is to mention successes, not fashion.

8. "I just heard . . ."

Gossiping in the office is a definite no. You don't want to gain a reputation as the pot-stirrer or a spreader of rumors or bad information. So, how do you separate acceptable conversations from the unacceptable? If you find yourself looking around and lowering your voice before saying "Did you hear . . . ?" the topic is probably off-limits.

Make Yourself Indispensable to Your Boss

The relationship between an employee and a manager is the professional world's ultimate two-way street. Your boss often acts as a mentor, opening doors for you and advocating on your behalf for a raise or promotion. Work to build a solid relationship and strive to be the type of staff member your boss would hate to lose.

Be at Your Desk on Time

This very simple gesture indicates you are reliable and take your job seriously. It doesn't mean spending the first twenty minutes of your workday retrieving coffee to wake yourself up, or putting on your makeup in the office bathroom. Once you walk through the door, be prepared to embrace your position's responsibilities in order of importance.

Maintain a Positive Attitude

Your demeanor can make or break your reputation around the office. Be known for having a friendly and courteous nature. When you're on deadline or stressed about personal issues, it can be an easy rule to forget. Your supervisor is keenly aware of your moods, and a consistently positive personality is something he or she can grow to trust and rely on.

Protect Your Boss's Confidential Information

Working closely with a CEO or other supervisor often means you will be cognizant of personal and sensitive information. It would be highly unprofessional to divulge private conversations, bank balances, client information or anything else that could tarnish your credibility as an honest and trusted employee.

Never Be without a Pen and Notepad

A creative entrepreneur is always thinking of new ideas. Be ready to jot down notes to use as reminders to follow up on at a later date. When your boss asks you a question regarding the conversation, simply refer to your notes.

Observe and Learn

You will gain important insight into your boss's work style by observing the way he or she conducts his or her daily business. You might notice the best time for a quick meeting is in the afternoon, or most of your boss's day revolves around sales calls and he or she prefers to compare calendars early in the morning. Study his or her habits and adjust your schedule accordingly.

Keep Up with Your Boss's Calendar

Staying up to date with your boss's itinerary is a positive reflection on you. Know where he or she will be, along with any important meetings and obligations that may require your assistance. Compare schedules at least twice a week to stay in sync. This routine will open the door to further discussions on upcoming meetings, projects and speaking engagements. Use this time to offer ideas, suggestions and highlight your efficiency, creativity and motivation.

Manage Yourself

On a day-to-day basis, nobody's in charge of your career but *you*. You have the power to increase your output, improve your attitude or knock the latest task out of the park. As a rule, ask yourself how you could do better and what will it take to make you stand out. Set goals against those ideas and put your thoughts into action!

How to Handle Professional Criticism

Accepting Criticism

No matter how fantastic you are at your job, at some point in your career, you will receive criticism. Perhaps it will come from a manager during an official performance review, or from an unhappy client or dissatisfied customer. Regardless, mental preparation enables you to receive criticism with grace.

Body language says it all

Criticism can be difficult to take in, and it's easy to immediately cross your arms, frown or furrow your brow. Think about adopting a neutral posture and remain relaxed. Place your hands on the table or keep them in your lap. Maintain eye contact, smile when appropriate and really *listen*. Pursed lips and eye rolls are a dead giveaway that you disagree; not a message you want to send to a boss.

Never make excuses

Placing blame on other people or circumstances is unprofessional. Avoid reacting negatively in the moment with an excuse. Instead, thank your manager for his or her insight and make it clear you plan to take those comments seriously. Schedule a follow-up meeting to talk through a plan and set goals for the coming months.

Don't brush off feedback

Even if you disagree with the critique, whether in the context of a formal review or a more off-hand comment or request, remain courteous and try to stay open-minded. Eager employees welcome the chance to learn and grow professionally. Welcome the opportunity to grow your skills.

Giving Criticism

Talk privately

As a manager, a primary part of your role is helping your employees succeed. That means assisting them, offering guidance and critiquing their performance. The number one rule: Talk privately. Never voice your concerns or speak critically of an employee in a meeting, in the break room or even with the door open. Address the problem head-on and be direct. Sugar coating the issue will be received as a weak management style.

Prepare your thoughts in advance

Structure your notes in a way that allows you to set the right tone for the conversation. If appropriate, include a positive thought about an area in which the person is excelling. If the issue is serious, get straight to the point. Deliver clear and concise information, giving specifics on what is expected and how the employee can improve.

Use "I" statements

Which would you rather hear from your boss? "You never come prepared to our pitch meetings" or "I've noticed that in our pitch meetings, you seem a little overwhelmed." Shifting the focus to the issue, and what you observe, helps prompt discussion and sets the stage for problem solving as opposed to blame.

Continue the conversation

Once you've delivered concrete ideas for how a person can advance, make it clear that you're available for follow-ups and you're willing to provide additional feedback as needed.

How to Ask for a Raise

Every professional needs to understand how to effectively ask for an increase in pay. Let's face it: In today's economy, workers often have to make the case for a higher salary—bosses don't tend to dole out raises with any regularity. It's worth noting, though, that a pay raise is generally based on your accomplishments and what you've achieved over the past few months (or even years), not on your personal needs. Improve your chances for a yes with the following tactics.

Become Familiar with Your Company's Policy

Knowing when you can anticipate a raise will give you a heads-up on *when* to broach the subject with your boss. Does the company tend to award a standard percentage after a certain period of time (for example, after one year of service, can employees expect a jump?), and is there room for negotiation? Perhaps raises are only awarded after annual reviews that take place every January. Knowing what to expect in advance will assist you in this conversation.

Do Your Research before Requesting a Meeting with Your Boss

Investigate what others are making in the same field. Make sure to compare equal tenure, experience, location and job perks, as these are all variables that can affect the bottom line.

Get Comfortable with Your Pitch

Make an appointment to meet with your supervisor and arm yourself with specifics on how you have brought value to the company at large and to your team directly. Be ready to offer facts and figures on how your performance as a key player has made a positive impact. Cite how you have, for example, saved the company money, built client relations and improved customer service. Prepare a checklist of positive undertakings you have been responsible for realizing, and leave this behind for your boss to review. Now is the time to market your skills.

Plan Your Reply

You may or may not receive a favorable response. Think through what you will say when your boss counters with a lower offer, or denies your request altogether. Always maintain a positive attitude, thanking him or her for the meeting and asking for some time to digest the conversation. Request specific details on how you can improve so as to secure a raise in the next earning period. Before leaving, schedule a follow-up meeting to discuss your progress.

Never Use Another Person's Salary to Justify Your Own Promotion

It's unprofessional to discuss salary with co-workers, especially if your boss finds out that you are using it as leverage. Not only will you miss an opportunity for potential growth, but you may stunt your career by conducting yourself inappropriately.

Rising Above Office Cliques

It's an unfortunate fact that most offices are populated, to a certain extent, by at least one clique, or close groups of friends who stick together in the office and socialize off the clock. Whether you're part of the gang, feeling like an outsider or you're a manager who's watching it all from above, there's a quick crib sheet for how to handle office cliques.

If You're Outside the Clique

When you're on the outside looking in, it's hard not to have a few flashbacks of high school insecurity. Even as adults, memories can haunt us. But if there was ever a time to rise above it and be the consummate professional (and, in fact, there are many times to do so), this is it.

If there are certain individuals you'd like to know better, on a professional or personal level, seek them out individually and suggest you have lunch or coffee one-on-one. Make time to expand your network in the office and be patient. Building solid relationships doesn't happen overnight.

Don't gossip or share secrets in an attempt to win an office friend's favor; this move always backfires and could leave you feeling even more out of the loop than before.

If You're Part of the Clique

Sure, it feels fantastic to toast to the success of a new project over happy hour with your favorite co-workers. But take a minute to look at the situation from another perspective: being mindful of those who might feel left out—for instance, colleagues who overhear you planning your next outing or group lunch but aren't invited, or associates who you're friends with on social media, and likely see all the pictures you post with other co-workers at dinner or sporting events.

Gossip is not respectful.

I also like to remind clients of that age-old idiom "You are known by the company you keep." Are there ways your involvement with the office clique could negatively affect your career? For instance, do they have one (or three) too many drinks at work functions?

Expand your network within the office. This will show your manager that you're inclusive and empathetic, and you'll build relationships with colleagues outside of your inner circle, which can only help you down the road. Of course, you're entitled to pick your own friends, but every so often, include your whole team in plans for lunches, happy hours or other outings. Lastly, when you're making plans with close friends at work (especially regarding after-work functions), keep quiet in the office and don't overshare on social media.

If You're a Manager

As the boss, your main focus is on your employees' work. But know that the environment in the office, and the cliques that form, can affect how well a person does his or her job. Be mindful, first, of how you interact with all your employees. Guard against showing any favoritism, especially when it comes to doling out projects or assigning particularly plum clients or new business.

Take the opportunity, as often as you can, to foster collaboration between departments and across the organization. Team-building retreat? Great. But if that's not in the budget, a group lunch or early-evening outing will do the trick. Fostering team spirit is an important part of leadership.

Love Thy Neighbor but Not Your Boss

It's not uncommon to have met the love of your life at the conference table, the water cooler or office kitchen. Dating someone you happen to work with means you already have a common interest or shared passion. But dating a co-worker can also be a minefield in terms of your professional growth within the company. Before jumping in heart first, evaluate the situation with a level head and proceed with caution.

Check the Policy in Your Workplace

Value your job? Read up on the company's rules before things get too serious. Plenty of offices are fairly relaxed when it comes to interoffice relationships, but others might have zero tolerance. You'll want to familiarize yourself with the regulations and what the procedure is for disclosure, should you need to chat with a superior about it.

Make Sure Your Manager Isn't the Last to Know

When and if you and your new flame decide to "go public," don't let your manager hear about it through the office grapevine. It's always better for your boss to hear it from you: Schedule time to meet, make clear that you've checked the company policy and assure him or her that you intend to keep your relationship discreet.

Be Inconspicuous

Even if it's public knowledge that you're dating a colleague, office displays of affection are disruptive. Even if your office friends are comfortable with your status, the tide can change in the blink of an eye when you get too cozy. *In the blink of an eye* is no euphemism here: Avoid any appearance of couple-love, including a flirtatious wink, a coy smile and certainly an unprofessional pat on the derriere as you pass in the hall. No need to hold hands in the break room or at the lunch table with your boss. Common sense must prevail in order for an office romance to work out.

Leave Personal Business at Home

Discuss your weekly shopping list, weekend wine tasting and summer vacation plans outside of the office. Wait until after hours to pore over house plans or pages on Pinterest of your favorite appliances. The less you include your peers in your day-to-day dealings, the happier they will be.

Think Ahead to a (Potential) Breakup

Nobody wants to consider the demise of a relationship while he or she's still in the early stages of a budding romance. But when you and your significant other work together, it's critical to walk through two hypotheticals: Say that you date for a while and things eventually fizzle out or, worse, turn sour. Will you both be able to remain committed to shared responsibilities or projects? And what if you continue down the dating path and "like" turns in to "love"? At what point would one of you be willing to look for a new position, either elsewhere in the company or at a different office altogether? These are important questions to consider before taking the leap.

Do Not Date Your Boss . . . Period

Doing so will, without question, damage your credibility with peers, reports and superiors. If mutual feelings exist, the two of you should discuss a reassignment to another manager, stat. Don't allow poor judgment to call your ethics into question.

If you're the boss, take heed. You don't want to hurt your employee's reputation or set him or her up for a rough patch. And, you certainly don't want to undermine your own professionalism. Do the right thing before moving forward.

And, Finally, Be a Trusted Co-Worker

If you come across an associate's or your boss's online dating profile, don't share it with the office staff. Everyone has a right to privacy and by announcing your discovery to others, you are showing you are not reliable with sensitive information across the board.

Office Meeting Basics

The act of running a productive meeting begins long before the group takes its seat. To host successfully, you'll need to prepare well in advance, arrive early, anticipate any problems or issues and follow up after the fact. Does this sound like quite a bit of work? It is.

The first thing on your agenda is to determine whether a meeting is necessary. Can you get expedient answers by email or a conference call, or quickly check in with your colleagues individually? The key is to respect everyone's time, so when you do call a meeting, all the participants will know that it won't be a waste of their morning. When a meeting is inevitable, observe the following rules.

Plan for the "Party"

And by that, I don't mean to equate your session to a bash. If necessary, sign up for a conference room that will comfortably fit your group. If there are twenty people who plan to attend, there should be twenty comfortable seats (not five around the table and five hugging the wall). If you need audio or visual equipment, make sure the room you've reserved has it—and that it works. Arrive ten minutes early to connect your device to the smartboard or other technology.

Articulate Your Goals

Begin promptly at the start time (stragglers will trickle in—and they'll learn not to make it a habit) and open with what, specifically, you hope to accomplish. Opening with your goals will help keep everyone on track.

Guide the Conversation

Some companies have more formal meeting guidelines, in which case you may need to circulate an agenda as your gathering approaches. Whether or not there's a written itinerary, make sure, as the host, that you keep the team on task. If anybody's going off the rails, transition with a phrase that acknowledges the point but refocuses the group, such as: "Absolutely, topic B requires careful consideration—so much so that I think it may deserve a separate huddle. For now, let's focus on topic A."

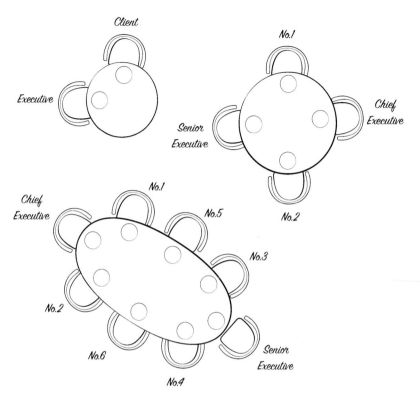

Seating arrangements are often made depending on company standings.

Enlist a Single Note-Taker

Most of us no longer operate in an environment where administrative assistants distribute minutes postmeeting. For an egalitarian way to ensure that everyone gets the necessary information, rotate note-taking duties around the team. Have one person mark down the decisions that were made—or the brainstorming ideas and content discussed—and email it out to the group later that day, or the next. This will help ensure everyone's not too busy scribbling to be truly engaged.

Watch Your Tone

As a leader, you bring much more to the room than covering the agenda and watching the pace. Your attitude is visible in the way you articulate your thoughts and in your body language. Do your best to put attendees at ease and welcome feedback. Trust that everyone will arrive prepared and ready to engage. You set the standard for success.

Always Follow Up

After the note-taker sends out minutes, follow up on any action items that surfaced. Check in with those who requested support and make a note of when to circle back around. Your diligence will pay off as you inch closer to company goals.

Set a Hard Stop

It goes without saying that you'll send an email or a calendar invitation designating the meeting's start time. Include an end time as well, so colleagues can schedule their day and manage their hours efficiently. Nobody wants an afternoon derailed by a meeting that drags on beyond its slated window. Have someone watch the clock and request a fifteen-minute warning to allow for pertinent questions before adjourning.

Body Language Basics

No matter how impressive your credentials, you could be sabotaging yourself with unintentional gestures and movements. When your mouth says one thing but the rest of you sends a contradictory message, it can seriously hinder your credibility. Minimize your misfires by making sure your actions are confirming what your mouth is communicating.

Unfriendly Handshakes

A lifeless grip communicates dishonesty, disinterest and insecurity. It is also downright unpleasant for the unfortunate person clasping your hand. A professional handshake should be firm, accompanied by direct eye contact and a smile.

Facing Away

When you are actively engaged in a conversation with someone, your entire body should face the person. If your torso or feet are turned away, you are saying, "I'm trying to escape," regardless of what your words are.

Crossed arms indicate a barrier.

Building a Barrier

Crossing your arms and legs is often done in the name of comfort, but it literally puts a barricade between you and the other person, sending a message that you are on the defensive. This body language says, "Keep your distance" or "I don't agree," indicating you aren't comfortable with the direction of the conversation. Make a point of uncrossing your arms and legs, and resting your hands on the table or desk to show you are relaxed and attentive.

Wandering Eyes

If you are talking with someone but your eyes are on your phone, the clock or the person standing behind that individual, you are sending a clear message that you are eager to say good-bye. Make direct eye contact approximately 40 to 60 percent of the time to let the person know you are actively involved.

Poor Posture

Your mother was right—you must stand up straight to make a good impression. Rolled shoulders, eyes looking down, conveys a sense of disengagement and leaves a negative impression on your client or boss. Stand tall, chin up, shoulders back, chest forward and look alive.

Fidgeting

Playing with your hair or twirling your jewelry undermines your authority and makes you look anxious. Break the habit before someone significant loses confidence in your abilities.

Cranky Resting Face

Some people's default expression is a menacing scowl, and they usually have no idea how they appear to others. Your grimace might be scaring clients away or giving them the idea that you are perpetually irritated. If your co-workers frequently ask if you are okay, consult a trusted friend about your "cranky resting face." Intentionally practice relaxing your eyebrows and jawline, adopting a softer, gentler countenance. You may find you will be asked out to lunch with peers more often.

9 Things Leaders Refuse to Do

Regardless of whether you are just graduating from college or running a large company, your choice to live life as a leader (or a follower) begins with your attitude. We have all met successful professionals who carry themselves with confidence and grace and wonder what it is they are doing right. Here are a few things they have shared to get you on the right path to success.

Leaders don't . . .

Leadership begins and ends with you.

1. Lose sight of their goals.

It's impossible to please everybody, and that's something leaders take to heart. Understanding that their goals will always evolve and change throughout time, they know how to evaluate what works and what doesn't. Leaders recognize that part of growth is flexibility and change. They welcome input from others but ultimately make up their own mind.

2. Allow boredom to take hold.

A natural curiosity and a sincere interest in others tend to spur leaders to think about the big picture, which means that while they might be working toward a few smaller goals, they've also got their eyes on what lies ahead. When a meeting gets canceled at the last minute, they use the extra time to catch up on a project or call a client they haven't talked to in a while. Leaders maximize their time and always look out for new pursuits, new opportunities and learning experiences.

3. Neglect self-care.

You can't lead (or at least do it well) when you're sick, tired or preoccupied. Leaders make their own health and well-being a priority, even if that means less time for work. They know when they turn their attention to their professional life, they are better equipped to perform. Leaders exercise, eat right and sleep well.

4. Rely solely on themselves for answers.

The staffing philosophy of most stand-up leaders I know is as follows: hire talented, driven people who are great at their jobs, then get out of their way. In other words, leaders play to their strengths but acknowledge that the strengths of others will only help them. Leaders don't take everything on themselves; they know that's unsustainable, and they'd rather focus their talents where they can make the biggest impact.

5. Rely on others' approval.

What do you imagine when you picture success? Maybe it's a high-level position at your firm or a job that lets you balance career and family. Perhaps it's a fancy sports car. No judgment! Leaders work toward their individual definitions of achievement, not society at large. There will always be someone richer, more attractive, faster, brighter—work on being the best you can be.

6. Trample over boundaries.

Let's face it: Great leaders can be tough bosses. They demand excellence and push their team to perform efficiently. But they also respect the people who work for them, and they recognize that nobody functions well when they're working around the clock. Leaders have their priorities in check and lead by example. They expect their employees to take time for themselves and not burn the candle at both ends.

7. Thrive on drama.

There are people who need a scene or a spectacle to propel them forward; these people feed off drama, and as such, they tend to create it wherever they go. Leaders don't get bogged down with gossip, rumors, or toxic people or environments. They won't be a part of it, and they expect the same of their employees.

8. Look back too often.

If you're stuck in the past, it's easy to obsess over previous mistakes or second-guess pressing decisions. If leaders make a mistake, they acknowledge that it happened, do whatever they can to fix it and move on. They live in the present and realize that no one is perfect. Mistakes lead to great lessons.

9. Ignore employees' strengths.

When some people begin to climb the ladder, they may see their employees as columns on an organizational chart or fields on a spreadsheet filled with salaries. Leaders remember the people who work for them are bright individuals who will be champions if they are acknowledged and rewarded. A leader knows the value of strong work relationships and does what is necessary to keep their employees motivated and happy.

Office Birthday Celebrations

An office birthday party can be viewed as either a nice break from the daily routine or a mandatory intrusion. No matter which camp you're in, birthday gatherings are often a part of the corporate culture.

View these occasions as opportunities to shine as you contribute in a positive way.

Honor Collectively

If you are in charge of acknowledging birthdays, consider a system where you celebrate on a designated day for everyone who will be turning a year older that month. Not many people like to be singled out, and by focusing on multiple people, you'll put everyone at ease. This approach also saves money and time.

Make It Brief

Begin the festivities promptly and keep them short. Pick someone who enjoys speaking in front of crowds and ask them to say a few words. Allow people to have a bite of cake, grab a drink and quickly slip back to their workspace without feeling guilty about getting back to work.

Don't Pressure Others for Contributions

If you're raising funds for an office-wide gift, know that not everyone will be comfortable giving. To keep things diplomatic, email the colleagues you'd like to include and mention that you'll set up a box or envelope in your office. Make the gesture voluntary and allow everyone to sign the card.

An Alternative to a Gift?

Offer to bring a food tray. Those watching their calorie intake will appreciate a delicious fruit salad or light dish. Another idea is to help with the setup before the party or to pitch in on the cleanup afterward.

Keep More Elaborate Celebrations Private

If you've decided to head elsewhere with a smaller group of friends after work, don't advertise your intentions to the entire team. For more selective outings, guard against hurt feelings by communicating outside of the office and keeping your conversations to yourself during work hours.

Receiving Line Etiquette

Are receiving lines out of date? We often see them at some weddings, but should they be used in business?

Absolutely! A receiving line facilitates introductions and serves an important purpose in large corporate and social functions, including cocktail parties and special events. And yes, of course, at weddings.

A receiving line affords the host(s) and guest(s) of honor the opportunity to personally greet and acknowledge each guest rather than trying to navigate through a sea of people.

It is an efficient way for important figures to greet each guest and allows attendees to be seen and noted.

In some cases, the host(s) may not know every guest. A receiving line ensures an initial introduction in a professional and hospitable atmosphere.

When and How to Use a Receiving Line

- A receiving line can make large business events and social functions (of more than 50 guests in attendance) run more smoothly.

- Charity events and weddings are perfect occasions for a receiving line.

- At a state dinner or political event, receiving lines are commonly used to introduce the guest(s) of honor to each attendee.

- The length of time a receiving line should remain in formation depends largely on the event size.

    A receiving line for a function of 600 people could last for 90 minutes.

    At a smaller event, the line may only be in formation for 45 minutes.

- **It is customary to exclude spouses from a receiving line in a business setting.**

    - Exceptions may be made when a guest of honor is accompanied by his or her spouse. The host's spouse stands in line after the guest of honor's spouse.

    - Example: Host is first in line, then guest of honor, then guest of honor's spouse, then host's spouse.

Setting Up a Receiving Line

- **Select a suitable location.**

    - The venue layout determines the optimum area to place the receiving line. Be sure there is adequate space for movement once a guest has greeted the host.

    - Place the receiving line away from high-traffic areas, including major walkways and the buffet, bar or tables and chairs.

- **Set clear expectations.**

    - A receiving line should be efficient but not feel rushed.

    - To prevent a potential standstill, position an aide nearby to encourage the flow, politely directing guests (as appropriate) to keep the line moving at a steady pace.

Going Through a Receiving Line

- **Keep it brief.**
  - Greet the host, say a few words and then move to the next person in line.

- **Clearly state your name.**
  - Although the introducer may present you to the first person in line, repeat your name to every person you meet. Be mindful of ambient noise and adjust the volume of your voice as needed.

- **Never go through a receiving line with a drink or food in your hand.**
  - It can be tempting to enjoy a drink or snack while you wait in a long line, but before you reach the host, place your drink on a nearby table.

- **Avoid line jumping. Even if the person in front of you is holding things up, be polite and wait your turn.**
  - You don't want the first impression you make to be pushy or aggressive.

Stand and Deliver

Introducing a Guest Speaker

Formulating the strongest way to introduce an audience to a speaker shows respect for the effort that went into what they are about to present. With your words, you are also helping to establish an atmosphere of professionalism and admiration.

Mention Your Association with the Speaker

When possible, the person who makes the introduction should have some type of familiarity with the person they are about to introduce. Make a personal comment, such as "I first heard Julia Jones speak five years ago, and I have been following her blog, along with her professional advice, ever since."

Make No Assumptions

Many names have varying pronunciations. When in doubt, double check with the speaker for the correct pronunciation. Stephan could be pronounced "STEE-ven" or "Stef-ahn" and it would be terribly inappropriate to mangle the speaker's name in front of a large crowd.

Practice Your Delivery

Just as good speakers should avoid reading their notes word for word, the emcee should carefully rehearse his or her introduction so as to deliver a seamless and conversational overview of what's to come. Too often, the introducer doesn't look at the bio until the morning of the speech. This sets the tone for a less than impressive welcome.

Anticipate the Speaker's Needs

Attention to every detail gives a speaker the ultimate environment for success. Ask the speaker if he or she prefers a podium or a table for written notes. Will the speaker bring in props or an electronic presentation? Does he or she prefer a lapel microphone or handheld? Water or hot tea? A successful setup is mandatory for a good outcome.

Set Up the Room Properly

If the speaker plans to walk around, make sure the seats are placed for optimum movement of the presenter. If there will be a large number of participants, how will the questions be accepted? Will volunteers be positioned in the audience with multiple microphones so everyone can hear the questions being asked?

Keep the Introduction Brief

Allow the speaker to deliver the information. Refrain from giving your own mini-tutorial before the presenter has had a chance to deliver his or her material. The emcee's job is to generate excitement, not give away the speaker's key points.

How to Deliver an Award-Winning Speech

Whether you are a seasoned presenter or are drafting your first presentation, there are three things a good speech requires . . . planning, preparation and practice. By the time you stand before your audience, you want to be intimately familiar with your material. How should you proceed?

Write It Down

Weeks in advance, draft out your speech and read it out loud to feel how the words flow from your mouth . . . Are you using words or phrases that trip you up? You may find some words are more difficult to pronounce and you may need to alter your verbiage. Writing something down is very different than saying it out loud in front of a crowd. Time your delivery and adjust it as necessary to the needs of the presentation.

Ask for Feedback

Present your speech to a trusted colleague, friend or family member. Ask for a brutally honest critique. It is better to hear feedback from someone you feel comfortable around, rather than test your skills on a crowd. Make adjustments based on their recommendations. Concentrate on speaking to your audience, rather than reading your notes. No one will know you are off track except for you.

Arrive Early

Do a microphone check and get familiar with the technology you will be using during your presentation. Find the person who will be introducing you to see whether he or she has any questions. Give them a copy of your bio in case they have left the one you sent on their desk at the office.

Turn Off Your Technology

Double check to make sure your cell phone and the alerts on your computer you will be using with your PowerPoint are turned off. Any ring, bell or whistle will be an invasive intrusion if it goes off in the middle of your speech.

Before You Go On

Do a vocal warm-up. Find a private area and rehearse your vowel sounds to get your lips and mouth ready to perform. Say A-E-I-O-U, repeating several times to exercise your facial muscles. You are ready to roll.

Start Out Strong and Confident

So many speakers walk up to the podium and blow into their microphone and ask, "Can you hear me? Hello? Hello?" Or say, "I'm so nervous, please forgive me." By doing this, you have already lost a few points. Get your audience's attention by asking a compelling question related to the subject matter, or tell a story that will break the ice. Unless you are a professional comedian, tread lightly with humor.

Understand Your Purpose

Are you there to inspire, inform, entertain or increase business? A good speaker will do it all. You demonstrate your credibility through your thorough knowledge on the subject, coupled with the emotional connection you are making with your audience. Draw on your own experiences and when applicable, give real-life examples of mistakes and lessons learned.

Use PowerPoint as a Side Dish, Not the Main Course

Nothing is more mind-numbing than reading a speaker's speech from an overhead screen. Don't overload your slides with numbers, charts and pie charts. Not only is it distracting and difficult to read, but it's frustrating and boring.

Know What Your Audience Is Looking for in a Speaker

The attendees expect to be informed. They stop listening when you ramble, mumble or your voice is shrill. They are also unresponsive to braggarts and sarcasm. They are receptive to a speaker who is pleasant, self-assured, appears genuine and speaks their language.

Close with a Call to Action

Encourage your audience members to stay connected to you by sharing your contact information and letting them know where they can find you in the future. Encourage them to continue the dialogue with you on social media or by email.

Office Technology and Social Media Savvy

There is no argument that technology is a priority in today's fast-paced business arena. However, there are circumstances where its use is not only a nuisance, but can also be rude.

The telephone may be one of the oldest items of office technology still in use. Interesting factoid: the first businesses to regularly use telephones were in New Haven, Connecticut, in 1878. Everyone knows how to use a phone—but do you use it to your advantage? Follow these simple steps to communicate effectively and appropriately.

- Your tone of voice creates a caller's first impression of you.
- Even if you're having the worst day of your life, smile when you answer.

There are a number of guidelines to help you avoid telephone disasters.

- Strive to answer on the first ring. No later than the second ring.
- Just as in baseball, three strikes (rings) and you're out!
- Answer the phone by saying, "Good morning (afternoon/evening), this is John Smith."
- Don't answer with:
    - "It's a great day—Lisa here."
    - "David here."
    - Or just "Hello."
- **Service with a smile.** A pleasant tone is difficult without curled lips.
- **Pronounce your words clearly.** Telephones tend to flatten a person's voice.
- **Don't keep someone on hold for longer than 30 seconds.**
- **Ask before putting a person on a speakerphone.** Let the person(s) know that others are present and will be included in the conversation.
- **If your call is disconnected,** allow the person who made the call to phone again. Even if the disconnection was your fault, stay off the phone for a few seconds to give the individual the opportunity to call you back. This rule of thumb alleviates confusion.
- **Return phone calls promptly.** Within the same business day is best, but not always possible.

Placing and closing calls seems simple, but remember to keep it professional at all times.

- When placing a phone call:
  - Make your own calls when possible.
  - Always identify yourself immediately.
  - Begin with your name, company and the person you are trying to reach; e.g., "This is Sue Black with XYZCorp. May I speak with Mike Smith?"
- When closing a call:
  - Follow up with a date and time for the next conversation (if appropriate).
  - The last words heard should be "Is there anything else I may do to assist you?" and "Good-bye."
- When leaving a message:
  - With a receptionist, ask for the best time to call back. Leave your message and the time you will try to reach them again.
  - With voicemail, state your name, number and the date and time of your call.
  - Briefly describe the nature of your call.
  - Close by repeating your name and number.
- Common voicemail mistakes:
  - Leaving only your first name.
  - Not including your telephone number.
  - Saying your number so quickly it isn't easily understood.
  - Starting your message with your name and number and then rambling on.
  - Not mentioning a time when you will be available for a return call.

- When returning calls:
  - Strive to call back within the business day. Someone at your office should follow up within 24 hours.
  - If you get a person's voicemail, in addition to your other information, leave a time you will be available for a return call.
  - If you must leave, or you get held up, a follow-up message with an alternate time is courteous.
  - **Avoid** calling or doing business with someone just before his or her office closes; you may only receive the person's half-hearted attention. If you must call at that time, be sure you have a good reason and get to business immediately.

Email is an important business tool. It can be your greatest friend or a dangerous foe.

- Its primary purpose is to expedite correspondence; eliminate frivolous conversation ("get to the point") and reduce the amount of paper shuffling.
- The body of an email (the message) is equivalent to a professional letter on company letterhead.
- Close the correspondence as you would a letter.
  - Customize your signature at the end of the message (between four and six lines).
  - Use your first and last name, company name and address, phone and fax numbers and email address.
  - Refrain from adding personalized quotes.
- There is no such thing as privacy.
  - Think of it as a postcard anyone can read.
  - Don't send anything you wouldn't want posted on the front page of your local paper.
  - Email administrators can read all messages.
  - Criticize in person, not by email.

- **Avoid** aggressive messages in ALL CAPS.
- Once you hit Send, a message is no longer within your control—it can be forwarded, altered or forged.

- Do's:
  - Fill out the Subject line briefly but with specificity—it gives the receiver the indication of the topic, and you will have a better response rate.
  - Begin with a professional greeting; e.g., "Dear John."
  - Utilize Spell Check and Grammar Check.
  - Blank lines help separate paragraphs.
  - Keep sentence length to 76 characters or less.
  - If forwarding a message, delete irrelevant information to shorten the email string.
  - **Always** look over your message before sending.

- Don'ts:
  - Send large attachments that have the potential to lock up a computer.
  - Email is not designed for essays—don't write them.
  - Overpunctuate!!!
  - Unless the message really **is** *urgent* or a *priority*, don't say so.
  - Use abbreviations and Internet jargon.
  - "Receipt Requested" can be misconstrued as mistrustful.
  - Send unsolicited mass mailings or spam.

Facsimile (Fax) Etiquette

- Always use a cover sheet that contains the name, address, date, phone and fax number of both the sender and recipient.
- Eliminate unnecessary pages and information—don't waste time and paper.
- Before you fax confidential information, call the recipient to alert the person that it is coming.
- It is an invasion of privacy to read a co-worker's fax.
- Use the company fax for business purposes only.
- To ensure your fax was received, make a follow-up phone call.

Social Media Etiquette

- Do's
    - Post discreetly.
    - Assume there is no privacy.
    - Avoid rants and steer clear from discord on a public forum.
    - Maintain a level of professionalism in your bio photo and information.
    - Understand that retweeting or reposting another's content may be interpreted as an endorsement of their views.
    - Ask permission before tagging a friend or co-worker.
    - Keep profile information up to date (including your current employer listed on LinkedIn).
    - Review your privacy settings regularly.
- Don'ts
    - Flood your friends' feeds with a flurry of updates.
    - Accept everyone as a "friend."
    - Request your boss or client become your Facebook "friend."

- Share personal updates while at work.
- Post controversial photos, use profanity or feel you must chime in on divisive topics.

Cell Phone Etiquette

- Power down or silence your cell phone during meetings, movies or any public event, including dates, places of worship and funerals.
- Texting and making or receiving calls at the dining table is intrusive and inconsiderate.
- If you must use your cell phone in a public setting, remove yourself to a private area.
- Do not shout or talk loudly into your phone; it gives the impression that you are calling attention to yourself.
- Don't violate the privacy of a colleague, client or friend by mentioning the individual by name.
- Don't discuss confidential business in public or a bathroom stall.
- Drive safely. Talking on the phone while driving is dangerous, distracting, and in most states, illegal.
- Before you start a conversation on a speaker, make sure your caller knows there are others in the room or vehicle.
- Avoid the whimsical jingle or barking dog ring sounds—the default tone is offensive enough!
- Wearable technology:
  - Silence smartwatch notifications before a business meeting or event.
  - Avoid the urge to constantly check your wrist for updates.
  - Stay away from voice commands in the office as they can be quite distracting.

More Tweet-Worthy Tech Tips

Social media opportunities are ever-changing, and it's difficult to write something today that won't be outdated in a few months' time. (What *will* developers think of next?) But regardless of which mobile video app or wearable gadget awaits around the corner, the rules for using technology with courtesy and respect remain the same.

Whether you're a super user (you just checked your texts on a smartwatch or commented on a friend's latest Instagram photo) or a casual-communicator (you'd rather "like" others' Facebook posts than write your own), take special note of the following tech tips.

Do Not, Under Any Circumstances, Vent about What Happened at the Office

Your Facebook feed might seem like the perfect outlet for complaining about a frustrating conference call or the fact that an officemate leaves moldy food in the communal fridge. Even if you're not directly connected with a colleague, you might have a friend in common who noticed the post and passed the sentiment along. Further, if you connect with your co-workers in the future, they might take a look back in time and find several of your less-than-polite missives. If you do mention work on social media, remain positive. A hiring manager might only be one post away.

When Attending Weddings or Other Special Events, Take a Pause before Sharing

Keep in mind the bride and groom likely hired a professional photographer to document their big day to avoid the poorly lit, unflattering, smartphone snapshots. If you're aching to share an update, post a photo of yourself at the event or a message wishing the honorees well. The only exception? If the ceremony or event signage touts a hashtag and encourages guests to start the conversation, feel free to post away.

Guard Your Online Image

Just as you want to look polished at a job interview, your image on social media needs to reflect the same brand. Start with a little recon: Scroll through your privacy settings across multiple platforms and make sure they are up-to-date. Untag yourself from any pictures you don't love, delete any tweets you might regret and be sure your profiles are helping you put your best foot forward. If a friend keeps tagging you in uncomplimentary photos, politely pull the person aside and ask that he or she please refrain.

Never Take Your Phone into the Bathroom

No big surprise, studies show that 75 percent of people take their device into the restroom, and of those, 87 percent talk or text from the toilet. It doesn't take a biologist to confirm this unseemly habit can result in the spread of bacteria. It also opens the door to accidental photographs . . . of you or others. Not to mention, it's unsettling to watch a co-worker holding a cell phone pre-hand-washing, only to then walk into a meeting and shake hands with clients and associates. The entire experience is unprofessional, unsanitary and unnerving.

Assume That Hiring Managers Search Social Media

Because more than likely, they do. Information that contradicts your qualifications could cause a problem and raise a red flag. Damaging posts include inappropriate language and such comments as, "It's Friday at 4:29 and I'm counting down the minutes to start my weekend." Clearly, posts about drinking or drugs are downright dumb! So, that selfie from Oktoberfest where you are wearing a beer stein on top of your head, which might have seemed cute at the time, is probably a poor choice for a professional headshot.

At the Office, Limit Your Browsing Time

Some employers block social media sites on office networks. If your company trusts you to manage your online networking while on the clock, be sure not to take advantage. Remember that checking in on Facebook, or using your phone to scroll through Instagram or watch a few Snapchats is a workday privilege. Keep your tech breaks short and concentrate primarily on your job. Use your social media wisely and you will have few regrets.

8 Rules for Getting Your Emails Read

Email is a necessity, but with the sheer number of messages we receive each day, it can quickly become overwhelming. It's increasingly difficult (and time-consuming) to identify which messages are really important, which are urgent, which can wait and what can be safely ignored.

That's why it's important to understand the rules of writing an email that is not only opened but read. Here are the eight best ways to make sure your emails get the attention they deserve.

1. Send judiciously

Build a reputation of sending emails with substance. If you routinely send correspondence that isn't necessary, such as "Got it," or "Thanks a lot," you are wasting people's time and setting yourself up to be labeled an inbox time waster.

2. Keep it brief

Get to the point and communicate as concisely as possible. An email that fills the screen with long paragraphs is daunting. It's easy to close an email with the intention of reading it later, only to forget about it as your day fills up with other tasks.

3. Let your subject line do the heavy lifting

Vague headlines invite others to ignore your message. Write a compelling headline that gets readers' attention and addresses the topic of discussion. However, don't veer so far in the other direction that you come across as misleading, tricking others into opening your email.

4. Respond promptly

A punctual response falls within the same business day. While appropriate times can vary depending on your workplace and the nature of the communication, make it a rule to reply to people as soon as possible. You are setting a precedent and giving others permission to respond back in the same time frame.

5. Timing is everything

No one wants to get an email requesting information at 4:58 p.m. on Friday afternoon. Not only is this an annoyance to the recipient, but by the time the person checks back on Monday morning, your message will be buried under an influx of other emails. Time your note so that those who get them will be receptive and ready to read them.

6. Avoid off-hours

Intentional or not, sending messages at all hours of the night and early morning implies that you are expecting an immediate response, whether it's five a.m. or nine p.m. If your goal is to show that you are so diligent that you're working around the clock, be careful—you are sending the message you are available around the clock. Similar to placing a phone call, be respectful of others' private time unless it's an emergency. If nine p.m. is the only time for you to send emails, schedule them to go out during office hours the next day.

7. Use "Reply All" with caution

Include only those who need to know in the back and forth correspondence. Being caught in an endless thread of meaningless emails regarding something that has nothing to do with you can be incredibly frustrating. Each recipient should only reply all when it's information that everyone needs (hint: it usually isn't).

8. Don't mark every message as priority

Save that red exclamation point for when you really mean it.

Virtual Meetings

In today's business landscape, worthwhile meetings don't require flying across the country or traveling around the globe. Thanks to modern technology, a sit-down with clients, colleagues or other stakeholders is possible with the click of a few keys, which is a huge plus for productivity.

When interacting with the help of a screen, it's important not to let basic meeting etiquette slide. Even if you're an A+ meeting moderator in person, you'll need to employ a few new skills to take your talent virtual.

Follow these rules for every virtual meeting, whether you're attending from a conference room or your home office, to ensure you will be a success.

Honor the Basics

With a teleconference, upholding the basic tenets of running a successful meeting become even more critical. Send out applicable information beforehand, start on time and outline any goals or objectives at the outset.

Manage the conversation in a way that keeps the group on task and lets each party report on his or her work or say what needs to be heard. Speak loudly and clearly and make sure to include virtual attendees.
Avoid side conversations with in-person counterparts.

Dress the Part

You should be as put together for a virtual meeting as you would be for an in-person gathering, particularly if you're joining from home. You may think your pajama pants won't be visible until you have a midmeeting emergency and need to stand up to retrieve a document. What's more, we tend to feel more confident when we dress for the occasion, so follow this rule of thumb regardless. (I suggest a similar approach for conference calls, as well.)

A virtual meeting requires office clothing from head to toe.

Get Familiar with the System

If a client regularly asks you to join in on Google Hangouts or chat on Skype, or if your company uses a certain software exclusively, take the time to learn how to host meetings, accept calls and so on. Even if it's not part of your job description, becoming fluent in the program will go a long way. For example, if you save the person who *is* running the meeting from an embarrassing incident, he or she will be forever grateful—and will likely repay the favor down the line.

Verbalize Expectations

Say you're presenting to a crowd on two coasts; request the participants mute their devices and make it clear that you'll ask them to unmute and open up the conversation for questions after each key point or during the final fifteen minutes of the call. Attendees will appreciate the guidance and the clear direction you are offering.

Keep Participants Engaged

With a virtual group, people tend to unintentionally talk over one another or interrupt. Circle back on points and encourage those who haven't spoken up to weigh in. After the fact, follow up as you would any other meeting with action items and next steps to those who are responsible. Don't sign off and assume your duties are done, whether you were in charge of the meeting or not.

Respect the Clock

If your meeting request stated the call would last one hour, make every effort to wrap up on time. If you have an especially talkative guest, step in and redirect to keep things on track. Covering information efficiently will be appreciated by everyone on the line, especially those who need to hop off for their next appointment.

Leaving the Company

How to Survive a Layoff

In today's work environment, the only guarantee in life is change. Thankfully, change is not always a bad thing. Looking ahead to an uncertain future can be scary, but take a deep breath and remember that your unemployment is only temporary. Brush yourself off and press forward with confidence. If you have recently been laid off . . .

Ask about Benefits

Larger corporations might offer outgoing employees an opportunity to meet with a career coach or attend a résumé workshop. In addition to inquiring about a severance package, be sure you know the policy on unused vacation days and the continuation of any benefits you received through the firm. When you receive the news, the HR department should have a packet full of information ready; carefully review it, and make sure you are clear on the agreement before signing anything.

Keep Things Professional

It could be tempting to hit happy hour with the gang and blow off a little steam. Remember that the network you've developed in this position just might help you land your next job. If you have one too many and complain all night about the boss, you are shooting yourself in the foot.

Give Yourself a Breather

It's okay to take a beat. In fact, I'd encourage it. Do what you need to mourn the loss of this particular job. When possible, block out a few days to get organized before you dive into a full-time job search. You'll be refreshed and able to put your best foot forward. Ponder what you'd like to do next; this can be an exciting time to research options.

Put Your Network to Work

Don't hesitate to reach out to your key contacts, friends and former co-workers who might be able to connect you with recruiters or pass on potential leads. Update your LinkedIn profile and other social media accounts sooner rather than later. Rest assured; hiring managers will check your credentials. Continue to attend mixers and introduce yourself to new people and opportunities.

Set Up an Interim Routine

Avoid sulking around in your pajamas and binge-watching on Netflix. Maintain a daily schedule. Get up every morning, exercise and take care of yourself. Invest time in an online class or develop a new skill while you are looking for employment. Research professional organizations (virtual or in person) that would benefit you to join. Soon you'll be back at work, and be disappointed if you don't take advantage of this time off to continue to improve your skills.

Keep an Eye on Your Finances

Post-layoff, when that severance check hits your account, it can be easy to continue spending money at the same clip as when you were gainfully employed. Realign your monthly budget with your new reality. While searching for a new job, pay special attention to superfluous expenditures. If you must spend? Invest in a new dress or blazer (on sale) for an interview or update your hairstyle to bring it into the current decade. Small investments in your professional appearance will make you feel confident and self-assured.

Job Search on the Job

In today's job market, it's not unusual for an employee to keep one ear and eye open for other opportunities that might pop up, even if they are happy in their current position. And while employers certainly value loyalty, they're also aware that employees are generally hoping to advance their career in one way or another, whether that's looking for a job with another company or in another field.

So, it's an accepted fact that, from time to time, an employee may be approached by a hiring manager or conduct a job search while gainfully employed. Keep in mind, there's proper job-search etiquette and professional guidelines to follow so as to avoid burning a bridge if you jump ship for another gig.

Guard Against "Checking Out"

Keep up the good work. You never want colleagues to get the impression that you're slacking off or getting complacent. And though you might be excited about a step forward, you need to keep your feet planted firmly on the ground. As much as possible, approach your day-to-day as if you're staying long term. Set goals and plan future projects. The average job search can take months and you don't want to set yourself up for failure in your current role. You always want to leave your position with a letter of recommendation and an unblemished reputation. Keep doing your job to the best of your ability until you walk out the door for the last time.

Keep It Quiet

If you're lucky, you have a few friends around the office. But even with close friends, take care when it comes to divulging your job search intentions. Yes, you might feel as if you're betraying their trust, but you don't want your boss to hear that you're leaving or looking from anyone else but you. And what if your peers are looking for a new position as well? They might already be going after the same listing, or might even jump on your lead.

Update Your Social Media Profiles

This is a general rule to uphold year round. When you accept a new position or receive a promotion, freshen your profiles ASAP. On LinkedIn, get active in the conversation among your peers and any groups you might be a part of, and keep the dialogue going. If you suddenly pop up on LinkedIn, while becoming more social on Twitter and other platforms, your boss will receive a pretty clear message: You're looking for a new job!

Avoid Utilizing Company Resources

This goes for printing out your résumé, nabbing envelopes from the supply closet or sending materials from the mailroom. Time is also a resource; don't scan job sites or set up interviews while you're on the clock. First of all, it's poor form for anyone you work with to walk by and see your résumé on your computer screen or overhear a conversation regarding your job search. But take the longer view: Does a hiring manager want to bring someone on board who corresponds exclusively during the workday or makes calls from their current office? No. Potential employers will imagine you're doing the same when you work for them.

Embrace Confidentiality in All Forms

Make it clear you're keeping your search private and ask the interviewer not to reach out to your current employer . . . yet. Don't tip your hat to the boss by wearing your best suit when your office is business casual, Monday through Friday. Finally, avoid posting your résumé to any job boards. Instead, work your network and apply directly for positions that interest you. As long as you are doing the right thing, and give your employer ample notice, it is your option to look for a new career.

When and How to Throw in the Towel (Quitting Your Job)

If you're itching to move on, it may be tempting to walk away and devote full-time hours to finding the perfect job. Not so fast! Moving full steam ahead on your career may seem like a smart move, but the truth is, employers would rather hire someone who's holding down a steady position than a person who quit prematurely (or was laid off or fired). It's always better to wait until you've ironed out all the details for your next position before you leave your current one.

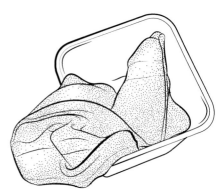

Let's fast-forward: You've just accepted a new position. Congratulations! I hope you take a moment to bask in the success of your job search and get excited about the fresh start and different role. But once the elation wears off, you'll realize that you still need to give your two weeks' notice. Don't even think about skipping this step.

While you're eager to wrap things up, keep in mind most bosses highly regard (and remember, down the road) employees who give appropriate time to find a replacement. If the situation allows you to provide three weeks' notice for special training, the gesture will be appreciated.

Maybe you love your job and adore your manager. Or perhaps the way the company's run is part of the reason you're leaving, and you're worried the boss might become combative or argumentative. Either way, handle the situation with grace, respect and professionalism.

Stay Positive

Set up a meeting with your supervisor and let him or her know of your plans to move on. Keep the tone upbeat, mentioning your gratitude for the opportunity to learn invaluable skills. When explaining to co-workers that you're leaving, don't complain about a colleague or discuss your dissatisfaction with the direction the company is taking. Make it a point to leave on a high note, showing kindness rather than discord.

Train Your Replacement with Integrity

Take the time to organize your files and put together a training manual. Ideally, you will have the opportunity to train your replacement personally, but leaving a checklist of important duties will be helpful for your predecessor once you are gone.

Adhere to Company Policy

Don't contact your clients without the seal of approval from your boss. If you receive the go-ahead, briefly explain that you will be moving on and reassure them they will be left in good hands. Let them know who they can contact to make the transition smooth for everyone involved.

Show Gratitude

On your last day, make time to say good-bye to everyone in the office you have worked with. Leave thank-you notes on each colleagues' desk or hand deliver a note to your favorite mailroom assistant. Don't wait for the good-bye party—bring in office treats for the group to enjoy. Leave the leftovers of your famous fudge behind for everyone to remember you after you have gone.

Remember, quitting a job doesn't mean it's necessary to sever a relationship. Continue to stay in touch with select office peers and your boss. There is a strong chance you will cross paths again.

The Delicate Art of a Powerful Business Meal

Dining Etiquette from A to Z

You are probably thinking, "I don't need to read this chapter; I already **know how** to eat!" If you are, then you're the ideal candidate for this topic.

Executive Dining Has Nothing to Do with Food!

It is no coincidence that second interviews and important first client meetings are often conducted over a meal. It gives the other person a perfect window in which to:

- Evaluate your social skills.
- Observe your confidence level.
- Watch how you handle an accident, spill or mistake.
- See how you treat the wait staff.
- Notice how you bring a fork to your mouth.

First Things First

- If you arrive before your client or an interviewer, wait in the lobby or by the reservation stand.

- Use good posture at all times, whether standing or sitting. No slouching.

- Turn off or silence your cell phone and put it way before you enter the restaurant. Check it only after the meal is over and you have said good-bye to your host or guest(s).

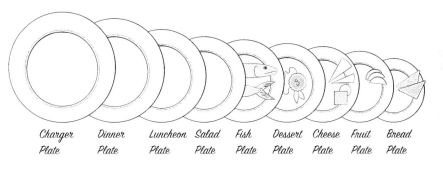

| *Charger Plate* | *Dinner Plate* | *Luncheon Plate* | *Salad Plate* | *Fish Plate* | *Dessert Plate* | *Cheese Plate* | *Fruit Plate* | *Bread Plate* |

- As you approach the table, remember that in business, both women and men seat themselves.

- At a dinner event (which is more formal than lunch), men should stand until all the women are seated.

- Approach your seat from the right, and take a seat from the left side of your chair.

- Keys, cell phones and purses don't belong on the table—put them away while being mindful to not invite theft.

- Don't hang your bag on the back of the chair, where it could cause a walking hazard.

- Men, keep your suit jacket on. Refrain from draping it across the back of your chair.

A basic table setting.

Conversation at the Table

- Discuss business after the drinks and appetizers have been ordered, allowing the host to lead the discussion.

- Socialize equally with guests on either side of you.

- Steer clear from controversial topics: politics, health and religion.

Napkin Etiquette

- Pause before removing the napkin from the table—follow the lead of the host or most senior executive.

- There is a difference between lunch and dinner napkins; the latter is often a bit larger. Don't tuck it in your belt, shirt or necklace.

- Napkins are not for blowing your nose!

- If you must cough or sneeze, do so into your left arm, facing away from the table.
- If you have a cold that makes a sneeze or a runny nose likely, stay home and send your regrets to the host. Reschedule for another day.
- When leaving the table for a moment, place the napkin on your chair and push your chair under the table.
- At the end of the meal, set the napkin back on the table before your departure.

Basic Primer

- Men, don't fling your tie over your shoulder or tuck it into your shirt.
- If you need to leave the table for any reason, a simple "please excuse me" is all that is necessary.
- Water and other glasses are placed on the right side of the place setting, above your knife and soup spoon.
- The bread plate is placed on the left side of the place setting, above your fork(s).
- Your salad and entrée plate is placed in the center of the utensils.
- Avoid chicken legs or wings, ribs, lobster, spaghetti and other foods that can be messy.
- There is no sharing of meals or "to-go" bags at a business lunch or dinner.

Soup Course

- Do not blow on or place ice cubes in your soup to cool it down.
- Spoon the soup away from you.
- Sip creamy or clear soup from the side of your spoon.
- Chunky soups are eaten from the front of your spoon.
- Between sips, rest the spoon on the soup plate, behind the soup bowl.

Spoon away to avoid dripping on your clothing.

- For a two-handled soup bowl and a bouillon cup, place the spoon on the saucer between sips and when finished.
- Never leave the spoon in the bowl or cup.

Bread and Butter

- Bread and butter should be offered to diners on each side before serving yourself.
- Pass to the right, counterclockwise.
- Avoid eating double fisted or swiping your bread across the butter.
- Break apart a piece of bread and butter one piece at a time.
- Never hold a drink in one hand and the bread in the other.

Salads

- Salads are a prime opportunity for an uncomfortable moment.
- Cherry tomatoes can explode or slide off the plate.
- Spinach and other greens can easily stick to your teeth.
- If you have the option, you may want to avoid ordering a salad and order soup instead.

Wine

If you are the host and have ordered wine, there are three things you should do when the wine is brought to the table: Look at the label to confirm it is the wine you ordered; look at the cork when it is placed in front of you to see that it is intact and not dried out; and taste the sample to make sure it is acceptable before it is served to your guests.

- Hold white wineglasses by the stem and red wineglasses by the lower half of the bowl.
- As a guest, if you do not care to drink wine, simply say, "No, thank you."
- If you are being interviewed for a job, decline liquor and choose water or tea instead.

Dining Styles: American and Continental

- American style involves switching the fork between hands as you use your knife to cut and then rest your knife on the plate. As such, there may be a great deal of noise and clanking.

- Continental (European) style requires you hold the fork in your left hand, the knife in your right. After cutting a piece of food, remain holding both utensils as you dine. The knife is used for both cutting and pushing food onto the fork.

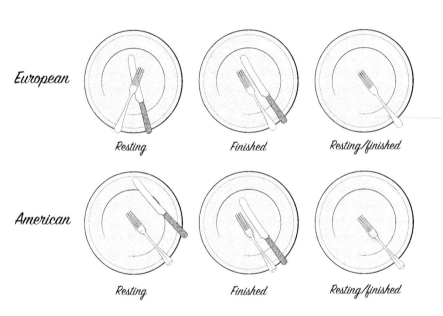

European

Resting   Finished   Resting/finished

American

Resting   Finished   Resting/finished

Table Tips

- Once you pick up your eating utensils, they must not be placed back on the table.

- The knife should cut the food behind the fork.

- When at rest, the blade of a knife is turned in toward the plate.

- Cut only one piece of meat (or food item) at a time.

- At dinners with multiple courses, sorbet (sherbet), also known as an *intermezzo*, is sometimes served after fish to cleanse the palate.

- Some dishes are served with a garnish, such as mint or parsley. The garnishes may be eaten.

- Watch the other guests' consumption of food so as to pace yourself accordingly.

- Gristle, bones and other foreign objects are removed with the fingers discreetly as possible, placing the item on the plate.

- See the diagram on the previous page for instructions and how to signal to the wait staff that you are either "resting" or "finished" with your food.

Finger Bowl Etiquette

For your fingers only.

While some people may never encounter a dainty bowl filled with warm water and a scent, it's a ritual that has been around for generations as a part of a traditional dinner service. In some situations, it is still in existence, and can actually be an interesting addition to a messy meal if you are familiar with how to use one properly.

On that note, here is a primer on finessing the finger bowl, just in case you are presented with the opportunity:

- A finger bowl will be brought to the table before the dessert course is served. The glass bowl is filled with water and includes a thin slice of lemon, used for cleansing your fingers before the next course. It generally sits on a doily, presented on the dessert plate, accompanied by a dessert fork and spoon.
- Dip only the tips of your fingers, one hand at a time, in the finger bowl. Take your fingers down to your napkin (on your lap) rather than bringing the napkin above the table to meet your fingers. Do not squeeze, touch or eat the lemon.
- After you have cleansed your fingers, grasp both the doily and the glass bowl together, or the individual glass bowl, and remove to the top left corner of your place setting (where your bread plate was placed before it was cleared for the dessert course). Bring your fork down to the left of your dessert plate and your dessert spoon to the right. You are now ready to enjoy your dessert!
- The bowl of water and doily remain to the left until the end of the dessert course.
- A finger bowl is not a sponge bath. It is not to be used for general cleaning of your ears, face or eyes!
- A modern alternative: Offer guests individual rolled, warm, moist towels after a messy entrée, served on a pretty tray. Pass the tray around to each guest, and then again to discard each small towel before consuming dessert.

Dessert

- Pie or cake may be eaten with only one utensil.
- Coffee may be served with the dessert course. If you don't care for coffee, a simple "No, thank you" will suffice. Don't flip the cup over as a sign you don't wish to partake.
- Keep your pinkie finger down when drinking from a cup.

Leaving the Table

- The host will call the meal to a close by wiping his or her mouth with a napkin.
- The napkin is to be placed to the left of the plate, or in the center of an empty place setting. Don't refold.
- Slide your chair under the table after you stand up.
- On your way out the door, skip the toothpick!

Duties of a Host and Guest at a Restaurant

A Sophisticated Host Knows How to Negotiate a Meal

- Your choice of restaurant is a personal reflection of your good taste; make a reservation at a restaurant where you are familiar with the menu.
- Mondays and Fridays are generally not the best choices, as guests are preoccupied with deadlines or tired from the long week.
- Consider your client's location when choosing a restaurant (where they are traveling from) and their ease of access to parking.
- Arrive early and make arrangements to take care of the check, tip, valet and coat check.
- Greet your guest(s) in the front lobby and allow them to walk ahead of you.
- Give your guest(s) the best seat at the table—facing the center of the restaurant.
- You are distinguished by the way setbacks, such as poor service, spills and mistakes, are handled. Complain away from the table or after your guest leaves.
- The person who extended the invitation (host) covers the cost of the bill, as well as leaves the tip.
- Gratuity is 18 to 20 percent for average service, above for great service. Never skip a tip.

Plates and Cups

Rimmed Soup Plate

Rimless Soup Bowl

Cereal Bowl

Cream and Soup Bowl

Boullion Cup

Finger Bowl

Breakfast Cup

Coffee Cup

Chocolate Cup

After Dinner Cup

Demitasse Cup

Well-Informed Guests Know They Have Responsibilities

- Your main goal is to show appreciation for the invitation.

- Order a mid-range menu item—not the least expensive and not the most expensive.

- Refrain from sending your plate back unless it's absolutely necessary.

- Act interested in others at the table.

- Ask questions and make conversation.

- Don't come across as high maintenance, making unreasonable or difficult demands. Exception: If you suffer from food allergies, you must articulate your needs.

- Thank your host and follow up with a handwritten note or email (depending on the formality and circumstances of the meal).

"After a good dinner one can forgive anybody, even one's own relatives."

—Oscar Wilde

Modern Etiquette for a Better Life

Navigating a
Buffet Line

Even the most sensible people can become raving maniacs at a buffet table. "Buffet" is **not** synonymous with "all you can eat!"

There are several things you should (and should not) do that will make the experience manageable and pleasant.

Do

- Survey the buffet beforehand.
- Start at the correct end of the table.
- Place your drink on the table where you will be sitting before approaching the line.
- Wrap the napkin and utensils in your left hand, securing as you hold the plate.
- Snack before you arrive. Contrary to popular opinion, you are not there to fill up on the shrimp!
- Take a small portion of what is being served.
- Keep your fingers out of the serving dishes.
- Make conversation with people in line.

Don't

- Overload your plate.
- Take two plates through the line.
- Expect gender privileges.
- Start at the wrong end.
- Hover over the person in front of you.
- "Graze" from the buffet table.
- Put your dessert on your entrée plate.
- Go for seconds until everyone has had a chance to go through the line.

A two-handed guest looks unsophisticated.

10 Foods to Avoid at a Lunch Job Interview

Meeting a potential employer for a follow-up interview is stressful enough. Factor in the pressure of a meal and you are prime for an awkward moment. Knowing what foods to steer clear from is half of the battle.

1. Spinach or kale salad

A light, sensible salad seems like a natural choice—until you realize you might have a dark-green leaf lodged in your teeth for much of the interview. Be mindful when ordering menu items that contain diced herbs or other ingredients that are ripe for sticking to your chompers. If you're worried this has happened, politely excuse yourself for a quick bathroom visit.

2. Pulled-pork or messy sandwiches

Are sloppy joes your ultimate comfort food? Come back another time to indulge. Sandwiches, in general, can be a challenge to eat gracefully if they're on a baguette or other hard-to-bite bread. Any food that's piled high on a bun with an inordinate amount of sauce will most likely spill onto your shirt and make a mess of your hands. Order with caution.

3. Anything requiring your napkin to be tucked into your collar

Baby-back ribs, lobster, crab . . . as a general rule, you should never order anything that might splatter or end up on your clothing. The only exception? The unlikely event your interviewer brought you to a crab shack or a rib joint and orders the goods him or herself. Consider this a green light to follow the lead of your host and feel free to "bib up."

4. Off-the-menu items

The fresh catch of the day, surf and turf, or other seasonal specials might sound oh-so-tempting. But chances are, they're also the priciest item on the menu. Avoid the urge, even if your interviewer decides to get one for him or herself. Nabbing the most expensive entrée is not using good business sense. Your prospective employer wants to get to know your social skills, not your high-end taste.

5. Cheesy soups

Soup is a smart selection, but your French onion potage will likely ooze with cheese and have you looking down the entire meal. Instead, choose a chicken chowder or lobster bisque, which are both easier options to eat with a spoon.

6. Spaghetti

If you've got to twirl it around your fork or suck it up through your lips, that pasta is a no-no. The likelihood of maneuvering your pasta into a mound the size of a basketball, then attempting to stuff it into your mouth is reasonably high. Opt for a penne or other small noodle that allows for smaller bites. Concentrate on maintaining a fluid conversation with your host instead of worrying about choking on your food.

7. Finger foods

With careful consideration, even a burger can be an acceptable option. But chicken fingers, shrimp tempura and other finger-licking, typically greasy menu options aren't a good choice for a job interview. By and large, you want a meal you can easily eat with a knife and fork. Your attention should be on the recruiter and their questions, not on the fries.

8. Something you've never had before

An interview over a meal is not the time to get adventurous. Don't try a new fish or a spice or decide it's your first chance to learn how to use chopsticks. The only thing you should "stick" with is something you are familiar eating.

9. Alcohol

At a job interview, even over lunch, politely refuse an offer of wine or liquor. It's best to go with iced tea, soda or water and say, "Thanks so much. I am going to pass, but please go ahead." You want to be at your best and are showing good judgment by taking the interview seriously.

10. Dessert and doggie bags

Don't assume you will be staying for dessert unless your interviewer takes the lead. Then, by all means, feel free to order the coconut cake or pie. And, never, ever ask for a doggie bag unless you plan on continuing the job search. Leave behind any leftovers, even if you would like to savor the remains for dinner.

The Importance of Lunch at the Office

In any work environment, the lunch break is full of etiquette landmines: There's the co-worker who inevitably microwaves a leftover curry dish or brings tuna salad that permeates the entire third floor. Or maybe a colleague who's an exceptionally loud chewer and eats hunched over his or her desk.

I don't need to tell you not to be one of those people. But perhaps you haven't considered the opportunities for networking and professional advancement that abound during a midday meal. Starting tomorrow, shift your frame of mind so you approach lunch not just as a quick break in the day and a chance to clear your head, but also as a window of time you can use to get to know co-workers in a different light. Put these work lunch rules into practice.

Always Take a Break

Even if it's just for 20 or 30 minutes. Lunch is a great time to step away from your screen (which includes your phone) and relax. So, whether you're sitting in the break room or cafeteria, or going for a short walk around the block or in a nearby park, make sure you build time in your day to actually

Use lunch to stengthen a bond.

use your lunch break wisely. Mindlessly eating take-out while trying to "catch up on email" means you'll overeat, begin the afternoon harried and miss out on a key slice of casual time you could be spending with peers.

Head to the Break Room

Ask if you can join a colleague you don't know as well, or invite others to dine with you. This informal time is a great way to build relationships outside your department, or even with your boss or direct reports. Keep the conversation light and upbeat and resist the urge to talk shop. If you're waiting urgently on an answer or a memo, mention it as you're both leaving the break room and heading back to your desk.

And Be Respectful of Everyone Who Uses It

Clean up after yourself. Don't leave items behind in the fridge (or take up too much room on a daily basis) and pick up your candy wrappers off the floor. Read carefully: If you nab the last cup of coffee, brew another pot.

Plan Ahead for a Lunch Meeting

If you're invited to a meeting over lunch, make sure you know the plan for the meal well in advance. If it's a bring-your-own affair, pack something that's easy to eat and doesn't have a strong aroma (a deli sandwich will fit the bill; fish stew won't). If a member of the team plans to order in lunch, be clear about any health-related dietary restrictions right away. Prefer not to eat onions? Just remove them from your salad or sandwich before you dive in. The fewer the requests, the less problematic you will appear. Bon appétit!

How to Propose an Eloquent Toast

The act of raising a glass and speaking comfortably to a group doesn't come naturally to most people. In fact, anxiety around public speaking leads plenty of men and women to ramble nervously when it's time to propose a toast.

Behind the most beautifully executed "Cheers!" is plenty of preparation and quite a bit of practice. Pull off a memorable toast with this straightforward crib sheet.

Plan It Out

Offering a toast is a thoughtful way to celebrate an accomplishment, acknowledge a friendship or honor a host for a fantastic meal. Treat your duty with respect by brainstorming well in advance of the event. Take notes on which points you'd like to hit and keep it short and sweet.

As a general rule, open with a quick thank you or introduction, make three main points and then conclude with the raising of your glass. Jot prompts on note cards and practice a time or two in front of a mirror. Run your toast by a trusted friend for honest feedback.

Stick to Water

Since most toasts happen at social occasions, be mindful of what you consume before it's your turn to speak. In other words, don't down that glass of champagne to combat nerves. Instead, have some sparkling water and a few appetizers and save the alcohol for after your brief dialogue.

Put the Knife Down

Clinking your knife against the side of your wineglass is not the best way to get everyone's attention. It comes across as a harsh introduction to a genteel occasion.

A better approach is to stand up with glass in hand and ask, "May I have everyone's attention?" It might take a few go-rounds, but continue standing, smiling and looking around the room. Once one person catches on, others will begin to quiet the crowd, and soon the rest will turn your way.

If you're toasting at a large gathering, ask that a few friends, colleagues or family members keep an eye out for this moment and help you silence the group.

Timing Is Everything

A host will make a "welcome" toast at the beginning of the evening, or at the start of dinner, once everyone has gotten settled. A second toast will be made by the host during the dessert portion of the meal to honor a special guest. The host makes the first toast; only then should a guest follow his or her lead. Feel free to toast the host for a wonderful event.

You're On

Speak loudly, clearly and most importantly, S-L-O-W-L-Y. Pause and take a breath after each sentence. And don't forget to smile! Make eye contact with the person you're toasting, but also look around the room to include the entire group. When you are finished speaking (45 seconds to a minute), make a closing statement, such as "Here's to Jeanne," and take a sip from your glass. The other attendees will then do the same.

The rule of thumb for a polished toast: Be bright, be yourself, be authentic.

Modern Etiquette for a Better Life

Negotiating After-Work Camaraderie (a.k.a., Happy Hour Fun)

Getting together with co-workers after a long day is an opportunity to mingle in a different environment. But before you order your next glass of wine, remember the emphasis belongs on the networking aspect of the experience.

When interacting with your boss and peers after hours, be mindful of the water cooler conversation that may follow the next business day.

Professional Mode: ON

A beer in your CEOs hand is no excuse to let your guard down or ask the individual questions about his or her recent divorce. Mixing business with pleasure can be a "perfect storm" or a chance to make a positive and lasting impression. You decide with each drink you order at the bar.

Snack Up

Make bar nuts, pretzels or whatever snacks available your happy-hour bread and butter. Before leaving the office, grab a small bite, such as a yogurt, an apple or granola bar. A late-afternoon treat will help you maintain your composure.

Drink Responsibly

Alcohol in any amount lowers your inhibitions. For some, even one or two glasses might result in them morphing from an intelligent colleague to a Sloppy Sam. Know your limit beforehand and adhere to it. For example, give yourself a two-drink max, and switch to tonic water for the rest of the three-hour event. Your drink allowance should be lower than what you might allow yourself at a friend's bachelor party. And, it goes without saying . . . don't overimbibe and get behind the wheel.

Switch Discreetly

Order a club soda or seltzer water and ask for a twist of lemon or lime . . . voilà, a "virgin vodka tonic." Other smart options include sparkling water with a splash of cranberry juice, or a diet soda and lime. When you are a great conversationalist, no one will notice you're not sipping a cocktail. Nor should you care if anyone does!

Wise Words

Even if everyone else is slurring his or her words, you are responsible for your reputation. Sip, don't guzzle and pace yourself. You will be glad you did. Cheers to a blossoming career!

Stemware Savvy

Brandy

Liqueur

Sherry

Martini

Highball

Pint

Dessert Wine

White Wine

Water

Red Wine

Champagne

Social Skills That Dazzle and Shine

Travel

Traveling with Your Boss

Travel is stressful enough, but when your travel companion is your boss, it can be downright traumatic. That is, unless you know what is expected and how to conduct yourself on the road.

A business trip doesn't have to be uncomfortable when you employ a few travel tactics.

Arrive First

At the airport, restaurant, hotel or meeting venue, get there ahead of schedule and scout out the lay of the land. Print off the itinerary before you depart and be clear on exactly where you are going, including addresses and names of clients you will be meeting with. You will appear prepared and on top of the situation, as opposed to keeping your boss waiting as you scramble for last-minute details.

Pack Light

Bring a roller bag or carry-on that doesn't require special attention. An overstuffed bag may be difficult to store in the overhead bin, and you could detain your boss while having to check it in at the last minute. On a flight with multiple layovers, include an extra change of clothing in case you miss a connection and have to stay overnight; one less thing to worry about!

Follow the Leader

Don't settle into your airplane seat and immediately put on your noise-canceling headphones. Your boss may want to talk business before or during the flight. If he or she pulls out a book or magazine, feel free to do the same. But be ready with a notepad and pen to avoid having to get out of your seat once you are airborne.

Don't Get Too Personal

You will have the opportunity to see your boss in a more casual atmosphere as you schlep through the airport and city streets together, but don't let your professional guard down. While you may have plenty of bonding time, sharing too much information about your personal life (if it's drama filled) may come back to haunt you.

Skip the Airport Bar

Unless suggested by your boss, killing time at the bar is probably not your best idea. One drink can easily turn into four, and you want to be alert at all times when representing yourself as a professional in front of your supervisor.

Select Clothes for Business, Not Pleasure

While you may be playing golf and enjoying some tropical downtime during your business travel, be aware of who might be watching. Save your tiny bikini or Speedo for the tropics and your friends. Choose loafers over flip-flops when traveling from plane to train and pack your suitcase with primarily business casual clothing rather than Hawaiian tropic attire.

Bring Enough Cash

The worst thing you can do is run short of money when you are far from home. Even when the company is covering all expenses, you don't want to be caught penniless in case of an emergency. While you are at it, check to see that you packed your driver's license and health insurance card. You will need ID if you fall off the curb of a city street and have to be taken to the ER—an unlikely scenario, but you won't regret remembering important documents.

Travel Checklist

Don't forget:

	Bathroom Essentials:
☐	Contacts and Solution (3 oz [90 ml] to carry on)
☐	Curling Iron/Straightener
☐	Deodorant
☐	Eyedrops
☐	Hair Products
☐	Medicines and Vitamins
☐	Razor and Shaving Cream
☐	Toothbrush and Toothpaste
☐	Sunscreen
	Electronics:
☐	Camera
☐	Cell Phone
☐	Charger(s)
☐	iPod/iPad/Laptop
	Travel Entertainment:
☐	Books
☐	Magazines
☐	Music
	Money and Documents:
☐	Cash
☐	Credit Cards
☐	Driver's License or Other Photo ID
☐	Insurance Information
☐	Passport
☐	Printouts for Hotel, Flight and Car Rental
☐	Printout of Travel Itinerary and Boarding Pass

	Additional Items:
☐	Hand Sanitizer
☐	Journal
☐	Snacks
☐	Sweater/Large Scarf/Shawl
	Taking Care of Business:
☐	When flying, check in 24 hours in advance and print your boarding pass.
☐	Get prescription medicine filled to last the duration of the trip.
☐	Have ample cash and traveler's checks.
☐	Keep a copy of the itinerary and emergency numbers in each of your suitcases. Leave a copy with a neighbor or close friend in case of emergency.
☐	When driving, make sure your car has been serviced prior to leaving.
☐	Send an itinerary to the host.
	Turn Off the Lights!
☐	Arrange for care of your pets and plants.
☐	Depending on how long you'll be away, consider halting newspaper, mail delivery and any other regular home delivery/care service (with the exception of lawn and pool maintenance).
☐	Close curtains and blinds and adjust the thermostat appropriately.
☐	Notify friends, family and a trusted neighbor that you are leaving.
☐	Remove all the trash and recycling from the house.
☐	Discard perishable food.
☐	Put your indoor and outdoor lights on timers to avoid the appearance of an empty residence.
☐	Double-check windows and doors and set the alarm.

Summer Makeup Bag Essentials

Ladies, keep a strategically filled makeup bag easily accessible at a moment's notice to ensure you will be ready . . .

☐	**Blotting Paper** – A must when temperatures start to rise.
☐	**Bronzer or Blush** – Make a light sweep over your checks on hot days or when going out with your friends after work.
☐	**Concealer** – Handy for everything from a quick touch-up to covering a blemish.
☐	**Comb or Brush** – To tame your wild locks after a breezy outdoor lunch meeting.
☐	**Eye Shadow and Liner** – When your eyes need a midday pick-me-up.
☐	**Hand Sanitizer** – Never leave home without it!
☐	**Lip Gloss** – A bare necessity when it comes to makeup, alone or over your favorite lipstick.
☐	**Mascara** – Reapply for a fresh evening look.
☐	**Powder with SPF** – A perfect combination for flawless skin and protection for your face from the sun.
☐	**Sunscreen** – Apply throughout the day. Cover any part of your body that comes in contact with the sun.
☐	**A Few Extras . . .** Safety Pin, Aspirin, Hand Lotion, Vitamin Pack, Favorite Scent and Mints.

Airplane Travel: First-Class Behavior in the Sky

Whether you're traveling for a business trip, visiting family or splurging on a much-deserved vacation, the process of getting through the airport—and surviving the flight—remains the same. These days, it's no easy process.

Develop a smart travel routine and you'll be prepared for virtually any trip in your future.

Devise a Travel Checklist

In a notebook or on your smartphone, make a list of all the items you will need for various types of trips. This could mean separate lists for a weekend at the beach or the lake, a business trip, a family vacation, an international getaway and so on. Now, half the work of packing is already completed, and you'll be ready to hit the road for a client meeting or weekend getaway at the drop of a hat.

Invest in Quality Luggage

A sturdy suitcase and a strong, lightweight carry-on will stand up to wear and tear for several years. Shop around for key pieces, watching for sales and special buys. Ultimately, all black bags appear the same; select gray, navy or bright blue for a quick-to-identify option that still looks professional upon arrival. Add a tag to easily spot your luggage as it circles the carousel.

Always Arrive Early

Pad your schedule to allow for emergencies, bad traffic, a long security line or other obstacles. It's better to have time to read a magazine at the gate or grab a cup of coffee than to run frantically through the terminal as the airplane door is about to close.

Be Considerate of Others

So much of the negativity surrounding airplane travel is about attitude. Rude passengers make for more rude passengers (not to mention the behavior puts a strain on the airline staff), so do your best to remain positive. Don't roll your eyes at parents traveling with young kids; when a fellow traveler asks to switch seats to be next to a wife, child or friend, happily trade spots. Don't wake your neighbor unless you need to get out to use the lavatory. Be patient when exiting the plane. The list goes on . . . play it safe and follow the Golden Rule.

Remain Calm

Your demeanor is especially important when it comes to interacting with airport and airline staff members. When a gate agent tells you that the overhead space is full, and you'll need to gate-check your carry-on, comply without a fuss. It's easy to snap at those delivering bad news, but a smile and a kind word go a long way.

Once, when traveling around Thanksgiving (a peak travel time across the country), I had seats at the very back of the plane. I approached the gate agent to ask whether my party could be seated closer to the front, as we had a tight connection at the next airport. Standing next to me, I heard a traveler speaking to another agent in a very rude tone. I apologized for all of the grouchy, weary passengers who were clearly not in good spirits. I kept my cool while the guy next to me sputtered on. As requested, our seats were changed a few seats up. Amazingly, when I approached the gate, I found my entire party had been upgraded to the front of the plane . . . a testament to "kindness counts."

A prepared traveler is a calm traveler.

Gratuity

Day-to-Day

- **Food server:** 18–20%
- **Food delivery:** 18–20%, minimum $5
- **Bartender:** $1 per drink
- **Restaurant valet:** $5 upon retrieval of vehicle
- **Stylist:** 15% of service
- **Shampoo attendant:** $3–$5
- **Manicure/pedicure/massage:** 15–20%
- **Flower delivery:** $5
- **Barista:** $1–$2

On the Go

- **Curbside check-in:** $3–$5 per bag
- **Skycap at the airport:** $1–$3 per bag
- **Taxi driver:** 15–20% of total bill
- **Shuttle driver.** $1–$2 per person
- **Limo driver:** 15–20% of total bill, check to see whether gratuity has already been included.
- **Hotel doorman:** It's not necessary to tip a doorman for holding open a door; however, if a special service is performed, such as helping with shopping bags from the taxi to the front desk, or offering an umbrella from the front door to the car, $2–$5.
- **Hotel valet:** $5 upon retrieval of vehicle
- **Bellman:** $1–$2 per bag
- **Concierge:** For directions, or simple questions about local sights or nearby restaurants, no tip is required. Arranging a dinner reservation, $5–$10. For hard-to-get tickets or reservations, $20 upward.
- **Hotel housekeepers:** $3–$5 daily, or $1 per person, per day, if there are more than five guests per room.

- **Room service:** 18–20% of bill, unless gratuity has already been added to bill.
- **Hotel spa providers:** 15–20%, unless gratuity has already been added to bill.
- **Pool attendant:** $1 per service
- **Hotel restaurant wait staff:** 18–20%, unless gratuity has been added to bill.
- **Buffet:** $2–$5 to the server attending your table throughout the night. For a large party, $1 per person.

'Tis the Season: Package Delivery

- **USPS:** Mail carriers may not accept cash gifts or cash gift equivalents. They may receive a gift valued up to $20.
- **FedEx:** Employees can accept a gift valued up to $75, no cash or gift cards.
- **UPS:** Allows drivers to accept a small gift or nominal gratuity, using their own judgment on what to accept.

Escalators, Elevators, Revolving Doors and More

Everyone is in a hurry, but knowing how to dash from place to place without knocking a person down or running someone over is worth the time it takes to slow your pace and arrive at your destination safe and unfettered. A well-mannered man or woman knows how to negotiate doors and walkways with grace.

Escalator

Stand to the far right of the moving stairs and allow those in a hurry to pass you on the left. If you are in a professional setting, and you are the person in charge, take the lead by stepping in front of your guest(s) to guide the way (both up and down).

Elevator

Allow those exiting the elevator to step out first. You may then walk into the elevator and move to the side, allowing others to step in behind you. If you are closest to the control panel, ask riders what button they would like you to push. Those closest to the door exit first, regardless of gender. Hold the door open for your guest(s) if they are carrying large boxes or luggage.

Revolving Door

Contrary to what would seem natural, the polite way to enter a revolving door is to step in first, saying, "Let me get this going for you," and lead the way. Never get into the same small area; allow the other person to enter his or her own section. Upon exiting your compartment, step to the side and wait for your guest before walking away.

Sidewalk Savvy

Pedestrian traffic has a flow, similar to driving on the road in your car. Just as you wouldn't drive on the wrong side of the highway into oncoming traffic, stroll courteously by staying to the right, "on your side." In heavy foot traffic, avoid a hard stop to take a picture of a landmark or tourist attraction. Keep your bags and umbrella close to your body and look left before taking a sharp turn.

Taxi

Never make your guest slide across a long cab seat. Hold the door, allowing your guest to enter the vehicle curbside and then walk around and get in on the other side. Or, if there is heavy traffic, step in first and say, "Let me get in first, so you don't have to climb across the seat." A guest wearing a skirt or dress will be grateful for the courtesy.

Bus, Train and Subway

When available, take a seat. If standing, hold on to a strap or pole, and offer your seat to the elderly, frail or those with a disability. Place your shopping bags on the floor to allow another passenger to sit down.

Doorway

In business, and in general, the person who gets to the door first should open it and hold it for the next person. This rule applies to both genders. When someone holds the door for you, don't forget to respond with "thank you."

Host and Guest Duties

Providing a Polite Powder Room for Your Guest

It's always a delight to walk into a well-stocked guest restroom and not have to "work" at finding basic necessities and small amenities. Here's a powder room checklist to make sure your out-of-town visitors (or an unexpected afternoon guest) feel welcomed with open arms:

Daily Essentials

- Plenty of toilet paper (no one wants to search for an extra roll in a pinch)
- A small waste can (with a liner, not a cast-off grocery bag)
- Decorative air freshener (placed on the back of the toilet)
- Fresh bar of soap (presented in the original wrapper)
- Liquid soap (an alternative to the bar)
- A box of tissues
- Finger towels (disposable)
- Hand towel on a hook

Modern Etiquette for a Better Life

- Magnified makeup mirror (standing or mounted on the wall)
- Night-light (to assist in finding the light switch in the middle of the night)
- Disposable mini drinking cups (for vitamins and meds)
- Full-length mirror (mounted on the wall or behind the door)
- Hooks (for wet towels and robe)
- Good lighting above a large wall mirror (over the sink)
- Fresh plant or small vase of flowers

Guest Niceties

- Blow dryer
- Hair spray
- Shaving cream
- Razor
- Toothbrush/toothpaste
- Small bottle of mouthwash
- Dental floss or picks
- Deodorant
- Elastic hair ties
- Aspirin/ibuprofen
- Bandages
- Cotton balls
- Cotton swabs
- Body moisturizer
- Earplugs
- Nail polish remover pads
- Nail file
- Antistatic spray
- Wrinkle-release spray

Creating a Welcome Guest Room

Do you get overwhelmed at the notion of hosting overnight guests? Setting up a guest bedroom doesn't have to be stressful, thanks to a few staple items that are easy to collect and pull together at a moment's notice. Offer family and friends a comfortable place to stay with your signature style and charm.

A luggage rack is a special touch.

- **Greet your guests with a beautiful vase of fresh seasonal flowers or foliage to brighten their travel-weary spirits and liven up the room.** Strategically place another small array of buds and blossoms in the powder room to add a special touch. If you have a green thumb, walk outside and pick your own blooms.

- **Watch the sales and invest in the best mattress you can afford, along with good-quality sheets, pillowcases and a couple of varieties of pillows to place on the bed.** Some people prefer a soft pillow; others, firm support. Avoid goose down in case your guest suffers from allergies.

- **Scent with caution.** Some people may enjoy a room freshener while others would prefer a more subtle scent. Place a candle on the nightstand with a pretty box of matches and let your guests know it's there for them to enjoy should they decide to light it.

- **Do a sniff test.** Pull out the blankets, towels and bedding. Make sure nothing smells old or musty. Now is the time to weed out torn or soiled items. Always launder guest linens and towels before company arrives.

- **Scale down the furniture and accessories.** The inclination to "more is better" is incorrect. In a guest room, less is best. Give your visitor plenty of room to walk around, remove multiple pictures from end tables and dresser countertops and clean out space for clothing in drawers and the closet.

- Offer a tray for keys and change.
- Include the Wi-Fi password on a note card, and leave it on a decorative dish for your guest to refer to when they want to send an email or check their social media.
- Set out a luggage rack.
- Reserve a place to store an oversized suitcase, preferably off the floor and in a corner of the room.
- **For guests that love to read, seek out a selection of their favorite reading material.** Place it in a basket by the side of a comfortable chair and make sure there is ample lighting.
- **No detail is wasted when you know someone appreciates your efforts.** Place a notepad, a pen, a few pieces of beautiful writing paper, an assortment of post cards and a roll of stamps somewhere your guests will find them. Let them know it's a gift for them to take home.

How to Host a Dazzling Dinner Party

You are hosting a party for out-of-town visitors. You are thrilled to introduce them to the rest of your friends and want to make the evening memorable. What can you do to awe and inspire the rest of your guests?

Allow Your Table to Shine . . . Literally

Nothing says you've cut corners like glassware and plates that aren't sparkling clean. There should not be a smudge or thumbprint on a fork, spoon or serving tong. Even if your dinnerware has been sitting safely on a shelf, give everything a quick swipe with a cloth after the table is set. Basic handling causes smears and spots.

Use Your Best and Borrow the Rest

For a special event, nothing but your finest will do. If your cupboard is limited, ask your family to share its inventory. Pull out your beautiful linen napkins, soak them in bleach, then wash and iron them to perfection. Make sure the fold is going the same way on each napkin at the table. If there is a monogram or design, place them uniformly at each place setting. Break out (no pun intended) your vintage champagne flutes and ornate wineglasses you are saving for a special occasion. The time is now; your pieces will never be called extraordinary if no one gets to see them.

Ban the Plastic

Just for tonight, veto the plastic pieces and disposable serving trays. Shine up your silver (or silver plates) and set them out on display. Allow your guests to help themselves to drinks from the crystal ice bucket, or appetizers, crudités and fruit served buffet style on serving pieces that are picture perfect.

Cover Your Table with Lovely Linen

Bare wood or cotton place mats at an elegant dinner party simply won't suffice. Roll out your beautiful table runner that was hand sewn by your grandmother or cover your table with a full damask tablecloth. Whether you choose one layer or two, the luxe material will add sophistication to your tabletop. Add interest and intrigue with special pieces that can double as conversation starters; for example, wineglass stem wraps or cocktail napkins that were given to you by your best friend when you were first married. A dinner napkin should be 18 x 18 inches (45 x 45 cm) to 24 x 24 inches (60 x 60 cm), as opposed to banquet napkins, which range from 24 x 24 inches (60 x 60 cm) to 32 x 32 inches (81 x 81 cm). As long as they are beautiful, either size will do the trick.

Set the Mood with Lighting

Have you ever noticed that guests tend to linger in your kitchen? Usually, the light is brighter than other areas of the home, feeling warm and inviting. Offer the same atmosphere to your living room, den and dining room by using soft lighting, strategically positioned throughout the rooms. Use floor and table lamps, chandeliers and votive candles to throw off a soft glow and allow your guests to illuminate to perfection. Switch out high-wattage bulbs for 40 to 60 watts and place mirrors to reflect the spark of candles and string lights, which are not only reserved for the holidays.

Plan the Perfect Playlist

During the cocktail hour, create a lively mood with modern, popular music. At the table, soften the music and play quieter, smoother notes that encourage group conversation. It's easier to chat with guests across the table when you don't have to struggle to hear them.

Assign Seating with Interesting Place Cards

Whether you choose to use gilded fruit or purchase pretty pieces of card stock, make the addition an eye-catching experience. Write their name on something that they can take home as a party favor, such as a mini bottle of champagne or a vintage compact for the women and a small antique box for the men.

Say It with Flowers

Have something fresh in every room for guests to enjoy as they stroll from the seating area to the bar, the powder room and back through the foyer. Once guests are seated at the table, a string of varying-size arrangements is more attractive than one larger piece at the center of the table. Use this as another opportunity to showcase your pretty collection of vases and vessels. A trailing garland from your local florist (or craft store) is another great option.

Start Your Collection

You only think about it when you need it, and after the party is over, you may not give a thought to your limited hostess supplies until your next soiree. Pull out a pad and pencil and make a list of what you are missing. When you find an estate sale, an off-the-beaten-path antique store, or someone asks what you would like for your birthday, pull out your list and give them a few ideas. You will grow your cache of party accessories in no time.

Modern Etiquette for a Better Life

Party Host Checklist

☐	**Dinner Utensils:**
☐	Forks (3) – Entrée, salad, fish (if you really want to get fancy, and who doesn't?)
☐	Knives (4) – Steak, salad, fish, butter (to be placed on your bread plate)
☐	Spoons (4) – Teaspoon, soup, coffee, dessert
	Dinner Plates:
☐	Service (also known as a charger)
☐	Dinner or Entrée
☐	Salad
☐	Bread
☐	Dessert
	Bowls:
☐	Soup
☐	Cereal
☐	Ice Cream
	Glassware:
☐	Juice
☐	Beer
☐	Champagne
☐	Martini
☐	Wine – Red and White
☐	Cordials
☐	Highball
☐	Brandy
☐	Shot
	Serving Utensils:
☐	An assortment of small cheese knives
☐	Large tongs
☐	Meat server (looks like a large fork)
☐	Serving spoons (looks like oversized soup spoons)
☐	Tomato server

Dinner Party Guest Faux Pas

A friend, colleague or acquaintance has invited you over for dinner. When you accept the invitation, whether by formal RSVP or an affirmative text message, you also enter into an unspoken social contract—that you'll behave like an A-list guest. Avoid these cringe-worthy blunders to ensure you'll build positive relationships and receive a second invitation down the road.

Arrive on Time

When it comes to dinner parties, there's no such thing as strolling in "fashionably late." Do your best to be punctual, within a reasonable five- to ten-minute window. Hurriedly bursting through the front door, with a bottle of bubbly in tow, isn't a good first impression for fellow party-goers just as they are about to enjoy the main course. Consider how you'd feel if you were forced to delay your scheduled meal for a latecomer, only to have other (hungry) guests linger while their food gets cold.

Avoid Monopolizing Someone's Time

The scenario starts innocently. You are engaged in great conversation, asking question after question, and suddenly cocktail hour is over and it's now time for dinner. A good guest understands the importance of circulating and meeting new people. Allow the host to greet and mingle with all of their guests and save the Q&A for a lunch or coffee date. Extend the same courtesy to fellow guests.

Don't Confuse a Social Function with a Business Gathering

You are not invited to a function for the purpose of pitching an idea or closing a deal. A social dinner party is not the time to float a new project or pester another guest for contacts or intel. You can absolutely chat about your career, and if you strike up a friendship, that's fantastic. But keep your business cards in your purse or pocket. It's bad form to pass them out at a social event. If someone asks for your card, discreetly oblige or simply say that you'll follow up with your information the next day by email.

Offer but Don't Insist on Hijacking Host Duties

Some hosts will appreciate help in the kitchen, while serving dinner or after the meal, during cleanup. Other hosts have a well-laid plan that doesn't welcome repeat inquiries of "How can I help?" Respect the "No, thank you," lending a hand only when welcomed. In the event of an emergency, don't reach for a pile of linen napkins to mop up that unfortunate red wine stain; ask which towels the host prefers you use (and retrieve them) before trying to save the day.

Follow the Host's Lead

Allow the host to propose the first toast. Don't jump out of your seat until he or she has a chance to propose a welcome toast or honor a special guest. Then you may follow suit, but only if you have something fabulous to offer.

Skip the Salt and Pepper

If it's on the table, go for it, but only after you have tasted your meal. Adding salt and pepper before the first bite is an insult to the chef. If you look down the table and can't find the shakers, don't ask. Either the cook believes the food doesn't need additional seasoning (in which case, asking for it is a bit of a slap in the face), or the shakers have been forgotten. In the latter scenario, not only are you drawing attention to the fact that the table setting is lacking, but you are also tipping off other diners to the fact that you think the food is spice challenged.

Taking a Phone Call

A ringing phone at the table is the ultimate offense. If you must take a call (one from the babysitter is an exception), set the ringer to vibrate and politely excuse yourself. Return within minutes unless it is a true crisis. Apologize to the host and fellow guests for the disruption.

Bon appétit!

RSVP
Etiquette

What does "RSVP" really mean? The word is derived from a French phrase, "*répondez s'il vous plaît*," which translates to "please reply" and the mannerly way to respond is with promptness! An expedient RSVP allows the host of the wedding, cocktail party or fund-raiser to formulate a plan, order food and contact the rental company.

Those who are respectful of other people's time are often the first to answer. How should you reply?

- Follow the directions on the invitation: Fill out a reply card, email your response or pick up the phone, depending on what the invite encourages you to do.
- Respond only for those who were invited.
- If any of the invited guests cannot attend, let the host know who will and will not be present.
- Don't assume you can replace one guest for another without the permission of the host.
- If you don't see your children's names on the invitation, you can feel quite certain they were not included on the guest list.
- Don't ask if your child may attend, which puts your host in an uncomfortable position.
- If you must change your response from yes to no, let your host know immediately by calling or emailing ASAP.

Here is an example of a courteous email:

Dear Jane,

John and I would love to come to your garden party. Thank you for including my sister Mary, but she will be out of town and won't be able to join us.

We look forward to seeing you on the 29th of May, at 3:00 p.m.

Sincerely,

Jeanette

How to Write a Notable "Thank-You"

Clients often ask if it's *really* necessary to write a thank-you note in today's always-connected, email–saturated world. My answer? A resounding yes. It's always necessary, whether you're showing your gratitude to a colleague or friend who went above and beyond their duties or writing to emphasize your enthusiasm immediately after a job interview. A thoughtful note will not only ensure that you're top-of-mind in the days following your meeting, but it could also set you apart in a competitive pool of equally qualified candidates. When it's time to put pen to paper, follow these simple guidelines:

Adopt a 24-Hour Policy

Have you heard the rule of thumb that newlyweds have a year to complete all the thank-you notes they should send after their nuptials? That statute of limitations is difficult to uphold when the gift giver is waiting for a written gesture of appreciation. Respond as soon as possible. Try your best to send out a card within a few weeks to a few months of receiving the gift. In business, a thank-you note should follow within 24 hours. Both a prompt and a tardy thank-you note will be observed and noted.

Invest in Good-Quality Stationery

Contrary to popular belief, a thank-you note—especially in a professional situation—need not be printed with the words "Thank You." You'll cover that in your handwritten message. For a more polished choice, purchase note cards with your monogram or initials. Write your note with a rollerball pen.

Start with a Rough Draft

Most of us don't write as much as we use a keyboard—at least beyond a chicken-scratch to-do list that no one else can read. Instead of jotting your thoughts down, free-form, start with a rough draft on a memo pad or piece of paper. This allows you to craft the ideal message and guards against running out of room or making mistakes that need to be fine-tuned. Once you're happy with your draft, write it slowly and neatly on the card, taking extra care to keep your lines straight and your words legible.

Get Specific, but Don't Get Too Flowery

If you're writing a post-interview thank-you, you need to make three main points: First, thank the person you're writing to for their time. Second, emphasize that you're excited about the open position; and third, reinforce why your experience and expertise make you a great fit for the position. In a personal thank-you note, make clear what you're writing about and why it was special. "Thank you for planning such a fun, relaxed and, above all, surprising party for my birthday!" says so much more than "It was so nice of you to plan a surprise party for me." In both cases, speak authentically and in your own voice.

Sweat the Small Stuff

Proofread your work, make sure you've spelled everything correctly, used proper punctuation and checked your grammar. Take special care when addressing the envelope and make sure your stamp (for a professional note, use a basic Forever Stamp) is placed on the envelope straight. From the moment the recipient pulls the note from his or her mailbox, this missive becomes an extension of your personal brand. You want all the details to exude your gratitude and grace.

Party Dress Code Defined

Black Tie

Men

A tuxedo. Period. Not a black suit—a straight-up, formal tuxedo.

Women

A long, elegant dress or separates.

Black-tie perfection.

Black-Tie Optional

Men

Wearing a tuxedo is up to you, but a dark suit and tie are required.

Please note, this does not include a tan or brown suit. Dark is black or the darkest gray in your closet.

Women

Either a long or ankle-length silk or sequined dress would be a perfect choice.

Alternative options include a fitted dress or very formal skirt that grazes the knee or above, worn with a beautiful evening bag, statement necklace or bracelet and a great pair of shoes.

How to Tie a Bow Tie

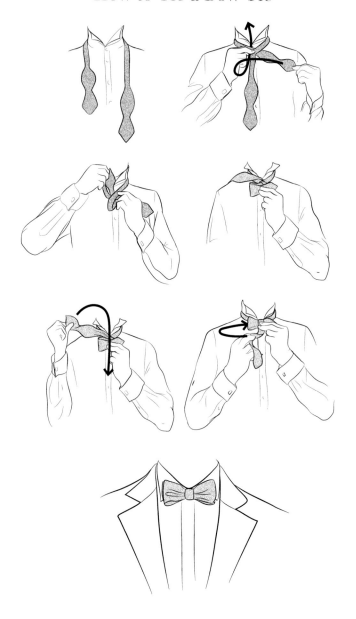

Black-Tie Creative

Men and Women

You are welcome to get imaginative with your choice of outfit. If there is a theme, incorporate something that depicts the era or focus. Texas Black-Tie would mean you could wear a beautiful dress with western boots (dressy boots!) or a tux and a western hat. Great Gatsby Black-Tie would require a sophisticated look, perhaps a vintage tux with a black silk tuxedo shirt for men, and all things beaded, metallic or velvet in a tiered dress for women. Have some fun and show up ready to win the "best dressed" award.

Cocktail

Men

Dark suit and tie.

Women

A dressy dress that hits the knee. For more conservative occasions, you can't go wrong with a classic LBD (little black dress) or an elegant dress with understated jewelry.

Business Casual

Men

Trousers and khakis with a sport coat are the standard, much to the confusion of those who think "casual" means jeans and boat shoes.

Women

A slim pencil skirt, or tailored slacks and a silk or cotton blouse, worn with or without a jacket.

"Dressing well is a form of good manners."
—Tom Ford

Hosting a Housewarming Party

Throwing your first party in a new place is such a fabulous way to show off your new digs—and, more important, send a message to family members and friends that your door is always (figuratively) open, and that you hope they'll return again and again. Whether you've just unpacked your last box and can't wait to unwind, or you're excited to see the new house your colleague's been raving about for weeks, here's everything you need to know.

Timing's Up to You

While most people throw a housewarming party shortly after they have settled in, don't wait too long. Even if every last picture has not been hung, allow your friends and family to celebrate within the first few months. The key is to be relaxed and ready to enjoy your new home, regardless of whether or not every last box has been unpacked.

Modern Etiquette for a Better Life

This Is Not a Time for Registries

A housewarming is not equivalent to a wedding or baby shower and does not warrant a gift registry. More than likely, your well-schooled guests will bring a small item for the house, although it is certainly not a requirement for entry. It's very bad form to make a gift request.

Flowers are the perfect way to say welcome home.

Be Prepared

Gather dining chairs, collect cushions from around the house and borrow fold-up chairs and small tables. Position them thoughtfully to encourage people to sit and enjoy food and conversation. Light the candles and outdoor lanterns and set up stations so that people can partake in different foods and beverages as they visit.

Do a Quick Run-Through

Since this is the first gathering at your new place, take a moment to think about specifics. View the party through the lens of a guest. Where will you place a trash can for bottles and plastic? Are the restrooms stocked with extra toilet paper? Will you establish a "shoes-off" household? If so, where will people put their Tieks? A new home calls for an updated routine. Use this as your initial launching pad for more events to come.

Plan a Great Playlist

Cultivate the mood with some upbeat music. A beautiful playlist comes to life with the help of a few wireless speakers. If you'll be streaming your favorite music service, upgrade to their premium version to ensure ads won't interrupt the atmosphere. Join in if guests want to dance.

Be Ready to Give a Spontaneous Tour

Inviting people over to see your new home means they will expect a bird's-eye view. Let them wander or give them a tour, even if you are not completely ready. Everyone will understand the moving transition and be excited to see how much you have accomplished.

And, a couple of thoughts for those attending a housewarming . . .

Offer to Help

Especially if the hosts are close friends, they'll be ever so grateful. Mention that you'd be happy to stock the bar as your housewarming gift, or that you could bring a pan of brownies, a plate of cookies or an appetizer tray. Volunteer to be the DJ for the night or tend the bar. Knocking a few tasks off the hosts' to-do list is a kind gesture they'll remember—and one they'll repay down the road.

Bring a Small Gift

A gift is not necessary but is certainly a nice idea. Here are some suggestions for thoughtful giving:

- A stylish welcome mat
- A good bottle of wine, cheese and fruit for the next day
- Monogrammed hand towels or etched barware
- A gift card to a kitchen or home improvement store
- A gorgeous coffee table book
- A potted plant

Talking Polite Politics

There's one topic of discussion that's hands-off in most business circles: politics. Technically, etiquette dictates that it's not acceptable to bring politics up at social functions, either, but the truth is, what's trending on the news is prime for conversation. In business, at a gala or with a group of friends over a burger and beer, adopt these winning strategies so you can walk away from any politically-charged conversation with your ego and relationship intact.

Realize Your Opinions Are Your Own

First things first: Understand you're not going to change anyone's mind. Talking about why you stand behind a particular candidate, for example, won't convince a friend who supports the opposition to come over to your way of thinking. Approach the conversation as a way to share information and points of view. You can disagree, and you will likely continue to disagree—but do it politely.

Make Sure You Know Your Facts

If you decide to engage in a conversation about politics, be certain it's an area where you can hold your own. A heated discussion can damage a relationship, especially when you appear uneducated and uninformed.

When in Doubt, Don't

Before you jump in to provide a counterpoint, consider whether the conversation is worth the frustration. Sometimes it's better to stay quiet, even if you strongly disagree with the statement an acquaintance is making or a stand he or she is taking.

Don't Misinterpret a Polite Nod as Agreement

For some people, it's easy to go off on a tangent when talking about an issue that's near and dear to our heart. So, while you might have a lot to say about how local politicians are handling—say, environmental initiatives—the person you're enthusiastically talking to might be taking the "hold your tongue" approach. Don't confuse a polite smile or nod as an invitation to ramble on.

Change the Subject

If a conversation is veering toward a charged political showdown, you have every right to step in and steer it elsewhere. And if the other party doesn't take the hint? Be specific and stand your ground. If a simple segue ("How about that game?") doesn't do the trick, feel free to be direct: "I know this topic interests you, but I'm not really comfortable discussing it. May we please change the subject?"

You Decide

Ultimately, you are responsible for what (and how much) you share. Reserve the right to stay and engage, change the subject, keep mum or even to excuse yourself and find another group of friends to visit with.

185

Weddings

Selecting a Dress to Attend a Summer Wedding

A Safe Choice

A long, flowy dress works effortlessly for both a breezy afternoon ceremony and an evening cocktail affair. Pretty flat sandals are the perfect touch for an outdoor occasion, while a strappy heel adds formality to a more conservative event.

Stylish Options

A knee-length dress is a nice choice when temperatures are high and the invitation says "cocktail." Choose a material such as satin or silk, as opposed to a summer-weight linen or cotton, which is more appropriate for daywear.

Color Play

A summer wedding soiree doesn't mean you have to stick to light colors or floral patterns. Bold hues make an entrance, but should not overshadow the bride. Steer clear of white or ivory, as they're reserved for the bride.

Shop Outside of the Wedding Section

Make sure the dress you select can be worn to other special occasions to get the most value out of your purchase. With a quick change of accessories, you'll have an entirely different look.

Make Sure Your Outfit Is Made for Dancing

Wearing something that doesn't feel comfortable will encourage you to leave early and miss all the fun. Try sitting and bending in your ensemble to ensure you can move freely and enjoy an extra piece of wedding cake.

Oceanside Ceremonies

A beach wedding calls for something that can potentially get wet and wrinkled. Heels are a "no-go" and an attractive shoe can be difficult to find when you will be trudging through the sand. Bare feet may even be encouraged, but remember that the sand gets hot! Give yourself time to locate the perfect pair, which should be both functional and attractive. A silver or gold slip-on sandal would be an excellent choice. Don't forget a gorgeous hat to protect your eyes from the sun.

Classic Black

Can you wear black to a wedding? The answer is yes if it's the right dress. Black can be beautiful for a festive occasion, as long as the outfit looks like it's meant to be worn to a celebration as opposed to a wake. Use a discerning eye and remember a mirror check before you say yes to the dress!

Food for Thought for the Bride-to-Be

We've all heard horror stories about demanding brides who think they are entitled to the ultimate wedding experience and expect their friends and family to cater to their every request.

Planning your wedding is one of the most important social events of your life. Keep things under control and maintain a happy relationship with your friends and family (including your bridesmaids) by establishing realistic expectations.

Don't Put Unnecessary Strain on Wedding Attendants

While it's customary for bridesmaids to pay for their dresses (and shoes) for the big day, keep their budget in mind. You are already asking them to sacrifice time, money for showers and travel if you are having a destination wedding. Don't anticipate they are happy to max out their credit card on a dress they may never wear again. Your friends love you and wish you the best, but also want to send their children to college or take a vacation, rather than dip into their savings account. Acknowledge they may have other financial obligations that take precedence.

Be Realistic When It Comes to Your Parents' Participation

If your parents have to take out loans to pay for your wedding, you are asking a great deal of them. People can—and do—have beautiful, elegant ceremonies that don't involve going into debt. Let go of over-the-top plans and stay within your budget. Assume nothing. Ask your parents what they are willing to spend, and be prepared to incur some of the debt if you and your fiancé(e) want a more lavish affair.

Treat the Vendors with Respect

If your caterer cancels your order or your wedding planner stops returning your calls, odds are you are driving people away with your excessive demands. Find highly rated, well-recommended people and trust them to do their job. Interact courteously and refrain from emotional outbursts. They want you to be pleased, but everyone has their breaking point.

Show Compassion for Unexpected Circumstances

Life happens. If one of your bridesmaids gets pregnant and must go on bed rest a month before your wedding, support her and let her know you understand. Some lucky bridesmaid may have two groomsmen instead of one with whom to walk down the aisle. You chose your wedding party because of your strong friendship; this is the time to show the love.

It Is . . . but It's Not Entirely All about You!

Chances are, your fiancé(e) probably has some ideas to contribute to the wedding planning. Set your life off on the right foot by making those wishes a part of the ceremony and reception. The day will be much more memorable when it includes the two most important people in the wedding plans.

The Perfect Wedding Guest

No social gathering is fraught with more etiquette landmines than the modern-day wedding. And with such a broad range of events (from formal church ceremonies to casual get-togethers outdoors), it's hard to know exactly what's expected. No matter how fancy or simple the affair, there are a few universal rules you must uphold as a courteous guest.

Early Is the New on Time

This basic tenet is threefold: RSVP promptly after you receive an invitation. For larger or more structured events, where the couple or parents must give the caterer a headcount in advance, there will likely be a date by which they need to hear from you. Most of us know, upon plucking the invitation from the mailbox, whether we're planning to attend. Don't wait—respond today.

Next, purchase and send the gift early. This will ensure you have plenty of options available on the registry, and it will cut down on the amount of bags and boxes the couple must move from point A (reception) to point B (their new home).

Finally, don't be late. Walking in as the bride prepares to make her entrance is not only awkward but disruptive. If you do arrive behind schedule, hang back and take a seat, quietly, in the back row once the bride has made her way to the front and the ritual is under way. It's best to arrive fifteen to thirty minutes early, accounting for unexpected delays and a crowded venue once you arrive.

No Surprises

Read the invitation carefully and if your name is the only one that appears on the envelope, it's only your shining face they want to see at the ceremony. If you are one part of an invited couple, arrive with your date (or your mate) and your dignity intact—not an extra friend or houseguest in tow.

Dietary Restriction Alert

It is your job to contact the couple about a dangerous food allergy. It would be uncomfortable to be seated at a formal dinner and pass on the meal because the caterer was unaware, and therefore unprepared, to accommodate your restriction. Some RSVP cards offer meal options, but in the event it is not included, reach out to the organizers early and let them know.

Post with Caution

Take a cue from the bride and groom when it comes to sharing on social media. If the couple has encouraged tweets and hashtags, go right ahead. But if mum's the word, do not post photos or details of the event prematurely. When in doubt, consult the bride and groom. Don't blanket Facebook with your fuzzy iPhone shots or tag others in unflattering photos.

Dress to Impress

It goes without saying; people will notice what you are wearing. Show your enthusiasm by selecting something appropriate for the time of day, climate and formality of the wedding. Use the invitation as your guide and when in doubt, dress up rather than down.

How to Have an Unplugged Wedding

All brides and grooms hope their wedding day will be perfect. That's why many couples are requesting those in attendance help keep the occasion technology-free.

It's an understandable move. With each guest carrying a smartphone, there are several ways a well-intentioned friend can cross the line into interfering with the day's events, from obstructing the professional photographer's lens to the phone ringing as the couple says "I do" (not to mention people trying to record the ceremony on oversized tablets or posting blurry photos on social media).

There is not a one-size-fits-all rule when it comes to technology at weddings, as there are many couples who actually encourage attendees to take pics, tweet, hashtag and share. But for those who want to minimize interference from technology, the following tips can help encourage cooperation.

Cell phone courtesy can be expressed subtly on a chalkboard.

Let Them Know in Advance

While it's not appropriate to include your "unplugged" request on the formal wedding invitation, do include your wishes on the wedding website and on tasteful signage at the ceremony (for example, "Welcome to Lori and John's Wedding. Please turn off your electronic devices before entering.") Assure everyone you will share photos as soon as possible.

Remind Them Again

Include a subtle reminder in the program. At the ceremony, have a member of the wedding party or the officiant make a quick, friendly statement just before the ceremony begins. Say, "Jennifer and Paul want you to share fully in the ceremony. Kindly silence your cell phones and refrain from taking or posting photos. Please allow the professional photographer and videographer to do their job."

Don't Attempt to Confiscate Phones

Most of us have a strong link to our phone. Many have legitimate reasons to keep it within arm's reach at all times, especially if the kids are with a babysitter. It's unrealistic to expect people to toss their phone in a basket or leave it at the hotel or in the hot car. Asking them to "check" their phones outside the entrance to your wedding is probably going to create more problems than it solves. So, make your wishes clear and trust your loved ones to behave accordingly.

Offer an "Altar Photo Op"

This is a simple option that will let people get the urge to snap photos out of their system. Once the bride and groom reach the altar, the couple turns around to face friends and family, the officiant presents them and invites guests to take as many photos as they would like to—then, they turn off their phones for the remainder of the ceremony.

Allow Photos at the Reception

While the ceremony may be off-limits for photos, you might enjoy the candid shots of friends and family that guests take at the wedding. Some couples even come up with hashtags for the sharing of photos online. Others ask to see the photos first, before posting or tagging.

Set Up a Photo Booth

Some couples let their guests capture the moment with a designated photo booth, complete with an array of festive props. There are thousands of ideas for this online, so find one that matches your style and theme and designate a corner of the reception area to indulge your guests. Again, give concise directions on what is expected.

Ask That No Photos Be Posted on Social Media

There are many reasons for this request. No beautiful bride wants an unflattering picture posted online for all the world to see. If an attendant posts a photo taken while the bride is getting ready, the thrill of the moment of the "big reveal" could be lost to the groom and wedding guests. Also, photos could create an uncomfortable situation for the bride and groom when viewed by people who weren't invited.

To all the guests preparing to attend a wedding, it all boils down to these simple words: **Respect** the couple's wishes.

The Role of the Mother-in-Law

When it comes to celebrating a loved one's wedding, everyone has a role to play. Siblings and the bridal party are often heavily involved, and traditionally, the bride's parents are special VIPs. How can a mother-in-law be most useful without coming across as overly assertive?

Follow the Happy Couple's Lead

The news of the nuptials isn't yours to share publicly until you get the go-ahead from the newly engaged couple. Ask them to let you know when it's appropriate to start telling your friends, family members and coworkers.

Build a Relationship with Your Counterparts

Now's the time to reach out and get to know the other set(s) of in-laws. Plan a lunch or dinner gathering where you can meet and get acquainted. Keep things light and casual, laying the groundwork for a lifetime of friendly exchanges. One day you will be sharing holidays and perhaps even grandchildren. It's always a good idea to proceed with general politeness and tact.

Offer to Lend a Hand

But don't be thrown off (or crushed) if the betrothed has it all under control. They might ask for your advice and input, but your son and future daughter-in-law likely have their own vision and might not welcome too much outside input (particularly from individuals who aren't footing the bill, which may or may not be the case). If you have a family tradition you'd like them to consider adding to the ritual, present it as a suggestion rather than a demand.

Wait Awhile to Choose Your Dress

Traditionally, the mother of the bride selects her dress first. Once you know what she'll be wearing, find something that's complimentary in formality and hue. You wouldn't want to show up in a brightly colored sheath dress if she's opted for a pastel cocktail dress. White and black are off the table unless specifically requested by the bride.

Meet and Greet at the Reception

While you aren't technically the host, don't feel as if you can't circulate, make introductions and introduce yourself to people you don't know. When you see an opportunity to help out (passing a message to the caterer, or rounding up a certain group for a photo), lend a hand. Your goal is to enjoy yourself, celebrate your adult child's wedding and make a positive and lasting impression on the family that's now merged with yours.

Wedding Registry Do's and Don'ts

Once friends and family get wind of your upcoming nuptials, the first thing they often ask is "Where are you registered?" Be ready and armed with information so you won't find yourself caught off guard.

Do

- Register early. After you announce the engagement, and start to plan your wedding showers, take some time to start your wish list.
- Offer gift-giving registry options. Although online shopping is convenient for most, there are still those who prefer to purchase a gift and hand deliver it. Register for a variety of items at different price points to provide guests with multiple choices.
- Be creative. If you and your groom are wine enthusiasts, perhaps a joint gift from your friends of a wine cooler or a monthly wine service would be preferable to a toaster or juicer.
- Include traditional items to your gift list. Aunt Martha may not feel comfortable funding your drinking, but would love to encourage your culinary talents with a bright-orange hand mixer.
- Link to your registry from your wedding website. You may want to consider a service that allows you to create one convenient online list with items from a variety of stores. Update your list when you think of things you would like to add.

- Keep a running log. And start writing thank-you notes as you receive gifts. Send the cards out before or the week after your wedding.

Don't

- Include the gift registry on your invitation. It's unsophisticated and very bad manners!

- Ask for cash. Tell close friends and family to spread the word if they are asked. Groom them on how you would like them to say it: "Jack and Lori are saving for a new home and would greatly appreciate a modest contribution."

- Use the gifts before the wedding. Call it superstition or simple common sense, but until you say "I do," keep everything in the box (and gift cards intact).

- Send electronic thank-you notes. Regardless of how progressive your guests may be, a handwritten note is the only appropriate gesture of thanks.

- Attempt to return a gift to a different store. Although it may be the same product, it's not ethical or polite to return something from another gift registry.

- Re-gift a wedding gift. Unless you are absolutely sure the giver won't find out and the person you are giving it to will appreciate and enjoy it. Never re-gift a family heirloom.

Other Social Events

Baby Shower Celebrations

What exciting news! A baby is on the way. There are countless options to choose from as you anticipate and celebrate the arrival of a loved one's child. It's a time to honor the soon-to-be parents, shower them with a gift or two and show them just how many people love and support them as they take this fantastic (and sometimes overwhelming) leap forward. Here's a snapshot of the types of events that fall into this category:

Gender Reveal

This gathering is a fun way to share the exciting news—a boy or a girl—with friends and family. Couples will ask their ultrasound technician to seal the gender of the baby in an envelope, and then bring it to a trusted friend (or neighborhood bakery) to have cupcakes or a cake made (with blue or pink icing piped into the center). Another option? Having a loved one fill a box with helium balloons and open the box at a designated time for all to learn at once.

Baby Shower

The most well-known celebration is the shower. According to tradition, a friend of the family—not an immediate family member—hosts the event. But the rules have somewhat relaxed, as sisters or even mom may be part of the host committee.

Sprinkle

If a couple already has young children at home, they don't necessarily need to be "showered" with gifts. After all, they likely registered and stocked up the first time around. A lighter shower, a.k.a., a "sprinkle," is an opportunity for friends and family to treat a veteran mom— and welcome her newest addition—while gifting her with a few items she might need.

An elegant gift for new parents is a classic mobile.

Sip 'n' See

Once the new family is ready to make their debut, they might invite loved ones over to savor a cup of tea or glass of punch and meet the baby. These gatherings are typically casual come-and-go affairs. A gift isn't necessary (but of course you will want to bring one). Feel free to call ahead and ask whether the new parents would like a frozen casserole, a basket of fresh fruit, warm muffins or something that can be easily heated and served after a long day or night.

Whether you're hosting an intimate gender reveal or a full-blown shower, the act of helping friends welcome a new baby is filled with potential etiquette missteps. Emotions (and hormones!) can run high. Follow these general guidelines to make sure everyone feels the love.

A few baby celebration tips for the host:

Paper or Paperless

It's up to you (and the guest of honor) to decide how the invitation is delivered. A beautiful card or a lively Evite® is perfectly acceptable. Alert invitees to any registry suggestions.

Involve Mom as Much as She Would Like

Once you throw your hat in the ring to host a gathering, inquire as to how much input the guest of honor prefers to offer. Ask whether she has preferences on a particular theme or color scheme. Or is she so busy preparing for baby that she'd rather show up and be pleasantly surprised by every last detail? A few things that are helpful to consider, either way: Would she like to play games? Are there any she has seen at previous showers that she loved or hated? Is she interested in a full meal at a restuarant or finger food in your living room?

Stick to a Budget

Decide in advance how much everyone is willing to contribute and be cautious of overspending. It's easy to get carried away, and some hosts may have to be more mindful of their finances than others. Don't overlook those who may be able to contribute time in lieu of money. Be open to new ideas and get creative with projects that don't cost a lot of money.

The 10 Commandments of Visiting a Newborn

What wonderful news! A friend just brought a child into the world, and you can't wait to meet the new bundle of joy. On this highly anticipated occasion, it can be difficult to contain your excitement. However, etiquette dictates that you must. This isn't your baby, so take a step back and consider the new parents, who are over the moon but sleep-deprived.

Commandment No. 1: Do not show up unannounced.

Unless you're the spouse or significant other, there is no open-door policy without an invitation. At the hospital or the new parents' home, always ask before you pop in to say hello. If dad isn't responding to your text message or email, don't assume it's okay to drop in. He's probably snapping endless photos on his phone, so he more than likely saw your message and is feeling overwhelmed.

Commandment No. 2: Go through the gatekeeper.

Before the baby's arrival, ask whether the mom-to-be has assigned a point person. Find out who you should contact to schedule a meal delivery or field questions. The first few weeks are usually a blur for new parents; they will soon welcome your help and an extra set of hands.

Commandment No. 3: Reconsider overly fragrant flowers.

Sending flowers to the hospital room or the new parents' home is a thoughtful gesture. Select a bouquet that doesn't have a strong scent; one with a heavy fragrance may have an adverse effect on the new baby or an overly tired and sensitive mom.

Commandment No. 4: Never assume it's okay to pick up the baby.

Wait until the parents ask whether you'd like to hold the baby and resist the urge to smother him or her with hugs and kisses. New parents are usually worried about germs, and it's up to you to understand their concerns. Avoid wearing heavy cologne and wash your hands in the hospital room before you touch the baby. Mom and Dad want to see the germs washed away.

Commandment No. 5: Be gentle and calm.

When you're handling the baby, be extremely careful. The parents are tired, fragile and likely feeling extremely protective. You don't want to overexaggerate your mannerisms accidentally and give them cause for concern. All eyes will be on you; keep things calm and quiet and avoid excessive rocking or jostling. Use a very gentle touch.

Commandment No. 6: Your advice is not welcome.

Do not offer your personal words of wisdom unless a new parent directly asks for it. What you did or didn't do is not important. New parents have their own way of approaching things, and they will learn what works and what doesn't as they go. Your good intentions to help will feel like criticism or control.

Commandment No. 7: Coughing? Sneezing? Stay away.

The new parents' top priority is to protect their growing family. Even if you know it's "just allergies," wait for a time when you aren't sniffling or showing signs of discomfort. It's much safer and more polite to be respectful of other people's qualms and feelings.

Commandment No. 8: Table the breastfeeding talk.

As you're cooing at a perfect, swaddled baby, you may feel the need to fill the silence with questions and comments. Breastfeeding is a personal decision and should not be a topic of conversation. If mom mentions it first, it's open for discussion. But if she doesn't, it's none of your business. Every parent gets to choose how they nourish their baby, and some women aren't able to breastfeed for a myriad of reasons.

Commandment No. 9: Make the siblings feel special.

Keep the older kids in mind as the family adjusts to its newest member. Offer to watch them or take them out for a treat, or bring them a new book or activity when you come to meet the baby. They're likely feeling a little bored (and maybe even a tinge of jealousy), so do the new parents a favor and help an older brother or sister feel the love. They may need a ride to soccer practice or dance class, and you can be of great help.

Commandment No. 10: Don't forget about dad.

More often than not, mom and baby get showered with attention while dad is feeling a bit left out. Bring dad his favorite bottle of wine or a basket with some comfort foods that he can heat and serve when he is awake with the baby in the wee hours of the morning. It doesn't take much to show your friend, cousin or brother he has not been forgotten.

Funeral Etiquette

Dealing with the death of a neighbor, friend or loved one is never easy, and there are often moments when you may wonder what to say or do. Knowing how to respond during this difficult time can offer some comfort to everyone involved. The following are some commonly asked funeral etiquette questions:

Q: *A distant cousin passed away, and I avoided his family at the funeral because I was at a loss for words. Now I fear they may think I am uncaring. Is there something specific I should have said?*

A: When it comes to expressing matters of the heart, there is no script. A genuine and compassionate, "I'm so sorry," or simply reaching out for a hug shows the grieving person you are touched by his or her sadness and attempting to show support.

Q: *Do I need to wait for an invitation to go to someone's home who has lost a loved one?*

A: When a friend or family member passes away, the family members of the deceased often feel overwhelmed with things to do. If you are a close family member or very good friend, by all means, pay your respects by stopping by the house. You can also offer to make calls, organize meals and document who has sent flowers or food. Every little bit helps during this sorrowful time.

Q: *Should I invite my ex-spouse to attend my father's funeral?*

A: It depends on the relationship your ex-spouse shared with your father. Would he or she want to attend? Do you two have children together? Even grown children rely on their parents for support. Are you remarried, and if so, how does your current spouse feel about your ex-spouse in attendance? Your husband or wife may have to put their feelings aside for a few hours for the sake of your children. Unless it would cause a major disruption, the answer is yes; you should reach out to your ex-spouse.

Q: Do I have to attend the religious ceremony of a deceased friend?

A: Similar to other occasions, such as weddings or bat mitzvahs, even when you aren't of a certain faith, it's a thoughtful sign of support to be present at the religious service of a close friend or family member. If there are circumstances that prohibit you from attending the ceremony, make sure and send a condolence card to the family.

Q: What do I include in a condolence card?

A: Don't overthink it. Select a card that expresses your feelings, mention how the deceased influenced your life and then follow with, "Sincerely," "Fondly," "Love" or "With Deepest Sympathy." You may also say, "My thoughts and prayers are with you and your family."

Q: My friend's mother died, and they are having a private service. I am not invited, but would like to drop by and sign the guest book to show my respect. Is this okay?

A: No, the registry is only for those in attendance. If an online guest book has been made available, feel free to use the space to express your condolences.

Q: What is more appropriate to send: food, flowers or a donation?

A: The answer depends on the particular family. Flowers are acceptable at most Christian ceremonies, but it would be in poor taste to send flowers to a Jewish family as a sign of sympathy. Nourishing, not festive, food might be more appreciated by a family that is sitting shivah. Some churches discourage excessive numbers of floral arrangements at the altar, or the family may prefer a donation to a worthy cause be made in lieu of flowers. The obituary often states the family members' wishes in regard to a donation.

Q: Is it better to have flowers sent to the funeral home or the house?

A: Again, there are no hard-and-fast rules on the preference of flower delivery. Sending flowers to the church is common, and following with a beautiful flowering plant to the family member would be a nice gesture. Keep in mind, flowers are not always welcome, and it should be left to the good judgment and discretion of the sender to determine which, if any, is the best route to take.

Q: I was left out of the family car at the funeral. Should I say something?

A: As difficult as it may be, try not to be offended if you were not asked to be included in the family car. There are a limited number of seats, and multiple cars may not be an option. Choose the high road and try your best to be understanding.

Q: Can I wear red to a funeral?

A: Red is highly discouraged. Although somewhat of a dated protocol, wearing a bright, bold color stands out and can seem disrespectful at such a somber occasion. I would strongly recommend you choose your wardrobe with the utmost respect for the family members and select a more muted color that shows deference to the departed. You can still be fashionable without screaming, "I'm here!" Dress options are more flexible for the celebration of a life.

Smart Tips for Daily Savings

Have you ever checked your bank balance and asked yourself where your hard-earned cash has gone? Or received a promotion or bonus, only to notice you are still short on funds by the end of the month? It's easy to make a quick purchase here or there and not give much thought to the bottom line . . . until you receive your credit card statement.

Positive self-esteem comes from making good decisions, and it's time to take charge of your finances, one day at a time. Pick a day and pay cash for everything you purchase. Log your expenditures in a notebook or on your smartphone. That evening, take a look at exactly where you spent your money. What habits can you change to put more cash in your wallet? Establish a few new routines that will enable you to live the life you're dreaming of down the road. Money in the bank brings more freedom and flexibility than a daily double latte.

Ready . . . set . . . go . . .

7 a.m.: Coffee Stop

Instead of popping into your neighborhood coffee shop, make your own cup of java at home. Do some research and invest in a coffeepot and quality beans that will inspire you to brew your own. We all have a jillion travel mugs that people give us as gifts. Pull one of them out and take a cup to go. Need more incentive? If you're spending $5 on a latte each workday, you're shelling out $100 month . . . that's $1,200 a year!

8 a.m.: Hit the Road

Sure, it's nice in winter to come home to a warm house (or a cool home in summer), but leaving your thermostat set to your ideal temperature when you're not around to enjoy it means you'll pay a premium on your monthly bill. Lower the dial in winter and crank it up a bit in summer, or consider getting a programmable thermostat. Strategically place a few small space heaters or fans for additional comfort.

9 a.m.: Operation Hydration

Spending a buck on a bottle of water at the vending machine doesn't feel like a huge expense, but much like your morning joe, this habit seriously adds up. Nab a reusable water bottle for work and to carry with you to the gym. Make it more exciting by adding lemon, mint or a flavor of your choice. Savings achieved!

Noon: Lunch Break

That $10 salad at a café near work is a healthy choice, so the cost may seem justifiable. But a years' worth of workday salads for $2,500 a year? Yikes. Stock your fridge and pantry with nutritious staples that will let you throw together a quick and easy lunch in the morning, such as a turkey sandwich or a vitamin-packed green salad. Take advantage of leftovers and bring extra to share with a co-worker. You won't feel as guilty eating out every so often when you are mindful of your budget most of the time.

3 p.m.: In Need of a Pick-Me-Up

Each week, bring a new batch of healthy snacks and stash them in a desk drawer. Have a nutritious bite when you are feeling an afternoon slump come on, or pop a couple of pieces of dark chocolate in your mouth instead of taking an afternoon stroll to the vending machine. Being prepared for hunger pangs is half the battle.

5 p.m.: DIY

Plenty of convenient services can be scaled back to an occasional treat. The superdeluxe car wash is almost as easily achieved in your driveway, and the weekly mani-pedi can be cut back to once or twice a month. The rest of the time, a swipe of nail polish remover, a great nail color and a file will do the trick. A weekly wash and blowout may be a luxury, but a color treatment for your hair is probably worth the monthly investment of a professional.

6 p.m.: Dinner Is Served

Cooking isn't just a basic life skill, but a therapeutic remedy for many people once they get the hang of it. If you are afraid of the oven, get familiar with some basic recipes or take a cooking class. Invite friends over and exchange food and recipes for the week. Browse Pinterest for inspiration. As your confidence builds, be daring. After a short while, you will love serving yourself (and your family) healthy, home-cooked meals. Your waistline will thank you, too. If you're pressed for time on weeknights, batch-cook a few dinners over the weekend and freeze. Thaw and reheat as needed throughout the week.

8 p.m.: Time to Start a New Book

Remember your local library? Yep, it's still there. And it still has books, magazines, CDs and DVDs . . . for free. And while purchasing material for an eReader is typically cheaper, know that most libraries offer services that let you download the same books straight to your device—sans late fees or the drive to the branch.

9 p.m.: Clean and Tidy

Ahhh, the day is done, and you toss your work outfit into a hamper, destined for the dry cleaner. Wait! Chances are your skirt, pants or blazer doesn't need to be dry-cleaned after every wearing. If you went through the day without any stains or spills, hang the outfit back up and get two or three more uses out of it. Not all clothes items require a trip to the launderer. Read the label carefully and decide which garments you can wash on the gentle cycle. Washing your white cotton shirts at home and giving them a good ironing is not only emotionally satisfying, it's good for your bright whites (which often turn yellow much faster after a few trips to the dry cleaner).

Thinking about all the money you are saving will continue to inspire you as you plan a trip or special purchase with a portion of the savings.

Don't
Settle for
the Scraps

I leave you with this final topic—because you can only do your best when you don't settle for the scraps. I received this question from a blog reader and I feel so strongly about this issue, I want to close with it. I share with you a universal truth:

Dear Diane,

I have been reading your blog for several years and I have always admired your ability to go from business to personal situations, hitting every mark. I would like your thoughts on how to handle a particular dilemma. My boyfriend and I have been dating for a little over nine years. We are not moving forward, and often take a few steps backward. He comes from a broken home and says that his childhood jaded him. He has a brother and sister, both happily married, whom he does not particularly care for. Both of his parents have also remarried and there seems to be no conflict among the exes. He has broken up with me several times to date other women, and I'm not sure I trust him, although he says he loves me. I don't have any close friends to turn to because I haven't had the best of luck with people close to me keeping a confidence, but they are good enough friends for now. I have two questions—is there hope for me, and what are the signs I am on the wrong track?

Suzanne F.

Dear Suzanne,

In life there is always hope, but the bigger question here is . . . is this guy worth the risk? That, Suzanne, I don't know, but based on your email, I can make a pretty good guess. I'm going to speak to you in broader terms based on your entire email, which I edited to respect your request.

After investing nine years of your time, in this and several of your other relationships, it may be time to wipe the slate clean. Start fresh. Dismantle any and all relationships that you have been accepting as "good enough for now" in the hopes that someday things will change. It seems that up until now you've been tolerant of the scraps, accepting whatever fate tumbles into your path like a fallen branch of a tree on a lonely road. To be clear, I think you have been **settling**.

What would happen if today, right now, you started fresh? If you made an effort to seek out specifically what you want, deserve and need? You have already started your journey by contacting me. I suggest you make a concerted effort to surround yourself with only people who promote your highest good. Seek those you trust, who share your joy and pain, openly express love and share mutual admiration and respect. Your choice of friends and romantic partner does not need to fall into a specific category: income, status, hair color, neighborhood or type of car they drive. The first criterion is they must be genuine and place the same value on you as you do them. As a matter of fact, from now on, make a promise to yourself not to settle for anything less. Even if it takes time—plan methodically and be patient.

Evaluate how you have chosen your relationships in the past. Chances are, many of your relationships have similarities. It's time to break the habit. No more excuses. Let go of, "He says he loves me but he's not ready," "She never asks how I'm doing but other than that, she's a really good friend," and "He acts this way because he had a bad childhood." Settling for second, third or fourth best is lazy and disheartening. **It's the scraps.**

If you have been waiting a very long time for something to take shape, and it hasn't happened by now, chances are the door is closed for a reason. Look for the reason you can't, or haven't, moved forward. It will probably be the same circumstances that it has been for the past nine years. The person who professes to love you doesn't have to convince you with words. You will know it—better yet, you will feel it to the bottom of your toes. If every instinct tells you to go, listen to your gut.

You asked me, "What are the signs you are on the wrong track?" Asking the question is one of the signs. You wouldn't have asked if you didn't wonder. If each interaction is fraught with conflict, tears and verbal combat, if every time he walks away you don't know if there will be a next time, respect yourself enough to kindly choose YOU.

Put your foot on the brake. Stop. Find another route. Begin to search for fresh relationships. Get a few new hobbies. Date a different type of guy. Close doors that don't lead to the opportunities you desire. Get out of your comfort zone and take a chance. Make room in your life for something great to happen. Robin Fisher Roffer, four-time author, and "fearless" advocate, says that what we do from the minute we have an instinct and when we take action can waste valuable time. Don't waste any more time.

One of my favorite symbols is the anchor, which signifies hope. But discernment and good judgment must be present. If you need help and guidance, find a professional to guide you over the hump and help you to see what you have been missing. The foundation of love is trust. You said you aren't sure if you trust him. Why not invest your time in someone you can always count on? YOU! Don't settle for the scraps—aim high and trust yourself. Settle for nothing less.

You are the master of your own destiny. The etiquette tips in this book were created for you to become the most powerful version of yourself. Settle for nothing less. I wish you my best!

References

Mann, C. R. 1918. *A Study of Engineering Education prepared for the Joint Committee on Engineering Education of the National Engineering Societies.* Boston: Merrymount Press.

Roffer, R. F. 2009. *The Fearless Fish Out of Water: How to Succeed When You're the Only One Like You.* Hoboken, NJ: Wiley.

Acknowledgments

Gratitude and Blessings

"And, when you want something, all the universe conspires in helping you to achieve it."
—Paulo Coelho, author, The Alchemist

Writing this book was on my to-do list, but the right opportunity and good timing allowed it to come to fruition at the appropriate stage. I am forever grateful to those who have inspired me along the way.

I was deeply influenced by my first boss who chastised me when he called me a "maverick," which only further fueled my fire to succeed; my beautiful mentor, now in heaven singing with the angels, who always encouraged me to spread my wings and soar.

To my amazing family and dear friends who have graciously allowed me to share my wisdom, even when they would have preferred to eat with their elbows on the table.

To one friend in particular who makes me laugh until I cry; another who appreciates and forgives my "unrealistic sense of urgency"; and last but certainly not least, the friend who taught me the value of perseverance and the art of balancing on a three-legged chair. My life has been made infinitely better for having known and loved all of you.

About the Author

Diane Gottsman is America's go-to etiquette expert, sought-out industry leader, accomplished speaker, television personality, author and the owner of The Protocol School of Texas, a company specializing in executive leadership and business etiquette training. Diane is the resident etiquette expert for *Good Day Austin,* a FOX News affiliate. She has been featured nationally on the *Today* show, HLN, Hallmark Channel, *Fox & Friends* and *CBS Sunday Morning.* She is an *Inc.* and *Huffington Post* contributor, and she is routinely quoted in such media as the *Wall Street Journal,* the *New York Times, Kiplinger's,* CNN, *Forbes, U.S. News & World Report,* the *Boston Globe* and the *Chicago Tribune,* to name only a few. Her popular blog, found at dianegottsman.com, consistently garners international attention.

She lives in Austin, Texas.

Index